NAVIGATING SOCIAL IDENTITY
A YOUNG ADULT STORY OF TIME

Juliet Dinkha & Aya Abdulhadi

Navigating Social Identity: A Young Adult Story of Time
All Rights Reserved.
Copyright © 2023 Juliet Dinkha & Aya Abdulhadi
v2.0

The opinions expressed in this manuscript are solely the opinions of the author and do not represent the opinions or thoughts of the publisher. The author has represented and warranted full ownership and/or legal right to publish all the materials in this book.

This book may not be reproduced, transmitted, or stored in whole or in part by any means, including graphic, electronic, or mechanical without the express written consent of the publisher except in the case of brief quotations embodied in critical articles and reviews.

Outskirts Press, Inc.
http://www.outskirtspress.com

ISBN: 978-1-9772-5918-9

Cover design by: Mennatallah Ali © 2023 All rights reserved - used with permission.
Photographer – Aya's portrait photo: Sarah Al Woqayyan © 2023 All rights reserved - used with permission.

Outskirts Press and the "OP" logo are trademarks belonging to Outskirts Press, Inc.

PRINTED IN THE UNITED STATES OF AMERICA

Acknowledgment

We would like to thank our family and friends for believing in us and for their ongoing support throughout this journey.

Thank you to all the contributing authors in the published articles, whose knowledge and experience were valuable to the making of this book.

Special thanks to the American University of Kuwait (AUK) for their support of Juliet Dinkha's academic interest and scholarship. The continued freedom to research without obstacles was possible only because of AUK's commitment to research.

Juliet Dinkha & Aya Abdulhadi

We spend our life living inside
a box of our own imagination,
to later realize we are only alive
when we set our 'self' free.

                                                          Juliet Dinkha

May you:

Leave no stone unturned,
no words unspoken,
no path untaken. Only leave
love and light behind.

Aya Abdulhadi

Preface

The idea of this book comes from living in Kuwait for an extensive period of time, which allowed us to be able to observe the interaction of young adults on a social level, and being able to examine the phenomena of their development through their lifespan. These observations were explored through methodological research and personal experience that we gained through interactions with the Kuwaiti youth, and being an academic in the field.

The Arabian Gulf remains an underexplored area in comparison with other MENA regions, and a book on Kuwait would be a welcome addition to filling this gap. The focus on a single country (Kuwait) as opposed to the Gulf may enable an in-depth exploration of a specific population, capturing the unfolding transformations. It is a laudable goal of the book to bring nuance into existing 'western' stereotypical understandings of Kuwait.

While gender segregation is an often-discussed topic, it is only controversial in moderation. Kuwait is a society seen as a partial freedom of expression and partial freedom of the press and encourages discussions that move society forward. This book explores aspects of how youth are socialized and how they frame and form their self-identity. Kuwait is a multifaceted society which is often misunderstood by the Western world as mired in a legacy of war, hardline Islamic values and oil. However, Kuwait is a sophisticated cosmopolitan where Islamic values mesh with Western ideals on consumerism, dating, media consumption and liberal arts education.

From gender segregation to social media, to body image, to altruism and gender roles, our book takes you into the world of the seldom explored lives of young adults in Kuwait. Driven by higher standards of living, today the youth and young adults are highly educated and have access to more disposable income than previous generations. This sets up scenarios where young adults seek out western media, foreign travel outside of the Arab world and study in foreign countries all of which are resulting in exposure to foreign ideals. This new milieu is a society comprised of European modernization juxtaposed with Islamic values. The youth are highly educated, technically savvy and politically sophisticated and are already re-shaping the economic, creative, and social dynamics of the society.

Through the pages of this book, we seek to inspire intellectual curiosity as readers navigate through it and discover the sense of self as it evolves within an ever-changing cosmopolitan society. The content shared will challenge stereotypes and bring awareness of the self, in relation to the social, economical and cultural melting pot we're exposed to.

Table of Contents

1. Introduction 1
2. Social Learning 11
3. Media Evolution 65
4. Coping Mechanism 183
5. Closing Remarks 236

CHAPTER 1

Introduction

THE CHAOS THEORY and the concept of the Butterfly Effect have given mathematicians and scientists a lens with which to view – and sometimes even discover – systems that don't seem quantifiable: large-scale phenomena that appear to have random origins or behavioral patterns, but in fact might be influenced by or operating according to unexpected common factors, attractors (Ghys, 2013). For psychologists and social scientists whose focus is the decidedly more qualitative, perhaps unpredictable world of humankind, the approach is still incredibly familiar. As humans we are united by universal notions and feelings, certain patterns of behavior and responses, but how each individual acts or reacts within the world around them can differ wildly from one person to the next. These differences can be the result of uniquely accumulated internal and external environmental factors that eventually shape a person as they are, maybe as they will become.

How different do you think you would have turned out in a different family, living on a different street, let alone in a different community, climate, even continent? On a more personal level, how differently do you think your life might have turned out given the sequence of events, decisions, and influences that have brought you to the present? Would one decision have made a difference, and could you ever begin to untangle what those sequences are? How much of the insights woven into your identity yours, and how much of them are really those of your family or your cultural circles? We can still better understand an individual's psychology when we take a look at the social sphere(s) they're immersed in, making connections and drawing insights from the findings. And it can help when we begin to find the dots that need connecting to start with.

Analyzing situations, seeking connections and deciphering signs is what makes us humans. This is how our brains function and interact with those around us. Understanding who we are and who we want to become is a lifetime journey which is often intercepted with various factors affecting its course, allowing each individual to create their own path in life. Some follow the footsteps of others (particularly those wielding influence, from parents to educators to social circles), some create new pathways and some trek in wander across various familiar paths to find their own route and identity.

Following the classic framework of the Social Identity Theory proposed by Tajfel & Turner (1979), individuals often try to categorize themselves and connect with others whom they think belong to the same circle, based on similarities in beliefs and ideations, such as religion, nationality, social class, etc. Once they've identified which categories they're most aligned with, they move to 'social identification,' adopting the ideologies and practices that mark said group. This is because they believe that this is who they truly are and where they belong, and social comparison helps them bond with others, cementing their place in certain groups as opposed to others. As this phase takes place, people continue to compare themselves and their groups to the other groups that they have identified, and actively identify differences that set them apart, while intuitively perceiving themselves as superior to the others.

The 21st century has seen the world undergo great flux, as nations continue to experience transformative changes in relation to their own identity and place in the larger global (globalized or post-globalized) community. Societies as a whole continue to engage in conversations about their collective identities and changing values across generations; in particular, it seems the headlines are often flooded with inquiries about who 'millennials' and 'Gen Z'ers' are, what they want, what they're thinking. Kuwait is no stranger to this, affected by the 'youth bulge' characterizing the whole Middle Eastern region and now more than ever at a crossroads between globalization, Western-centric soft imperialism, and the conservative values of a slowly-changing local culture.

Kuwait at A Glance

Kuwait is a Gulf country situated at the upper point of the Persian/Arabian Gulf, neighbored by Iraq to the north and the Kingdom of Saudi Arabia to the south, one of the six members of the Gulf Cooperation Council. The nation-state is governed as a constitutional monarchy, gaining its independence from Great Britain in 1961, having already produced oil since the early 1940s. Kuwait's society largely comprised pioneering businessmen and merchants, fishermen and pearl divers, who pride themselves to be Kuwaitis, forming a conservative and closed society with Islam as the leading religion of its people. Soon after the economical boom and the need to outsource talent in vital fields such as education and medicine, Kuwait became the home of a number of expatriates of select professional skills. Kuwait continued to be a country of trade in the region due to its strategic location and explored different economic growth opportunities. The Iraqi invasion of Kuwait took Kuwait by surprise in August 1990, and soon after, the countries' bilateral relations may have been restored over the years. However, to the people of Kuwait who experienced this trauma, things have never been the same since. Today, Kuwait's society still continues to be closed and conservative in essence, although its people are evolving as with any society. The people continue to allow and adopt different ideologies and concepts in pursue of a better Kuwait, which ultimately affects the overall social framework of the society. The population of Kuwait is dominated by expatriates, both Arab and non-Arab and both professional workers and domestic laborers, while Kuwaitis constitute around 31% of the current population of 4.2 million people (Central Statistical Bureau, 2018).

Kuwait's Collectivist Society Explained

While Kuwait is regarded as a collectivist society in essence, as most of the Arab and Far Eastern societies, the people of Kuwait are becoming more individualist, compared to the old Kuwait. Collectivist societies tend to favor the interest of a group over oneself, and this is greatly influenced and enforced by the Islamic religion, which is widely practiced by the people of Kuwait. In collectivist societies, the 'others before me' concept is the first thought adopted at any decision making process (Turner, Hogg, Oakes, Reicher & Wetherell, 1987). Consideration of family name and reputation, maintaining a social status ('what will people think?') tend to influence decisions that are not decided on the family level. Kuwaiti society has been greatly impacted by the effects of globalization, largely attributable to the government's approach of subsidizing its population, enabling them to be exposed to new ideologies and practices at home and abroad. The Ministry of Education in Kuwait ensures to provide merit-based academic scholarships to Kuwaiti high school students, to pursue their undergraduate studies abroad. Generations of families received their education outside Kuwait, and it is now a norm for young men and women to study abroad before returning to Kuwait post-graduation. Few, however, choose to remain outside Kuwait to pursue a career, and as a result, are denied certain privileges which they were to receive if employed in Kuwait. The access to an abundance of social welfare benefits created by the government, monetary amongst others, allows Kuwaitis to become frequent travelers to the rest of the region and beyond. With travelling comes the window of exposure to different societies, and adopting different practices follow. Upon return to Kuwait, certain western ideologies remain practiced and applied in Kuwait, particularly those propagated as part of Western-centric media, consumerist behavior, and others, all of which enriches the individual. They may find their sensibilities changing, with new approaches and ideas becoming part of who they are and how they interact with others. Extended families tend to engage in similar activities and practices, including travel and education, and when the new ideologies are adopted by an individual, this also influences other family members. Hence, certain foreign behaviors start to become acceptable among their closest social circle, and this then further expands with a rippling effect. The Kuwaiti society includes a substantial expatriates' presence, which also induces the exposure to various ideologies and practices introduced by both Arab and non-Arab foreigners who are in constant interaction with the locals in certain spheres of activity, whether at school, at work, or in the marketplace.

Gender Differences in Kuwait

Societies and individuals are normally identified by their ethnicity, names, language and culture. However, modern societies are increasingly expressing concern in losing their identity by the adoption of what are perceived as foreign cultural beliefs notions of gender equality and freedom for women. Given that the societies we live in, are and will most likely remain patriarchal for a long time. We all want to be identified with something or somebody and these forms of identification are often patriarchal whichever way one looks at them. As long as we all want to be identified with somebody or something patriarchal, it will be very difficult to achieve gender equity and rid our societies of discriminations against the "weaker or fairer sex". If there had not been historical universal gender inequalities, there would not be an ongoing battle for gender equality. That is why gender discussions is really about acknowledging the rightful existence of women in society.

People often define themselves socially according to how they relate to their primary culture, religious affiliation, gender identity or sexual orientation, citizenship status, and even socio-economic class. Gender identity is one of the most prominent statement for young people in Kuwait as they maneuver through their different social roles and expectations. Women's identity construction in relation to gender is closely tied with the quest for independence, and to show their capabilities without the male counterpart.

Gender segregation (that is, the separation of boys and girls or men and women in social or educational milieu) has been in the Arabian Gulf for decades. There is research in support of segregation all over the world, however, this type of segregation in Kuwait is starting to be seen as a serious issue in relation to one's identity.

If gender segregation was more prevalent and commonplace in the Gulf of the past, many of Kuwait's young people find it less acceptable. Females are more often opposed to gender segregation than males, mainly because males often benefit from segregation and maintain superiority over females. Gender segregation exacerbates women's struggles to a healthier balance in social rights, and that's why they continue to demonstrate their independence at every opportunity possible, to prove to themselves and the society how they are capable of being independent. Though some research have purported gender segregation has been effective in terms of schooling, the opposing research shows its detriment. Furthermore, it has also been shown to be detrimental in social and racial issues, as well as in breaking gender stereotypes and creating a sense of cohesion in Kuwait's communities and society as a whole (AlMatrouk, 2016).

Kuwaiti Youth and Young Adults

Like much of the Arab world, over the last several decades Kuwait has experienced a significant youth bulge, where those under 25 account for 30.1% (The Public Authority For Civil Information, 2022). Driven by higher standards of living, since the discovery of oil in the 20th century, modernization of the country and standardized education, today Kuwaiti youth and young adults are highly educated and have access to more disposable income than previous generations in a relatively rapid span of time. Setting up scenarios where young adults are seeking out English-language Western media, foreign travel outside of the Arab world and study in foreign countries, all of which are resulting in sustained exposure to foreign ideals and values. Some have described this new milieu as a society comprised of European modernization juxtaposed with Islamic values (Alsuwailan, 2006).

The influence of the youth bulge in Kuwait can be demonstrated with the 2005 law granting women full political rights including the right to vote and run for elected office. Observers describe young people as mobilized, coordinated, and able to use their technical expertise, often circumventing official media channels, to spread awareness and to ultimately effect wide-sweeping change or at the very least engage in national conversations. This has included a recent push for reforms that confer greater power to the democratically elected parliament.

On the whole, the youth in this region are highly educated, technically savvy and politically sophisticated and are already re-shaping economic, creative, and social dynamics of the society. And as this develops, we anticipate that the country's young people will increasingly place pressure on society to self-reflect and adjust to meet the changing socioeconomic demands and expectations of this population.

What we present in this book is a closer look at the social identity of youth (ages 17 to 34) in Kuwait, both Kuwaitis and non-Kuwaitis, and how this identity is realized in today's world, amidst changing social mores and expectations; increasingly connected and diverse media consumption; cultural, generational, or gender differences; limitations; and societal privileges, all of which presents nuances that belie the country's size and challenge outdated perceptions of a more static, homogenous population. The collection of articles in this book represent research conducted in Kuwait between 2012 and 2020 examining questions within social psychology, communication, and sociology that tap into the many elements impacting young people in Kuwait. How do young people in Kuwait understand, experience, and deal with mental health issues, body image, the impact of adversaries, such as COVID-19, on their everyday life? How does broadcast and social media impact social cohesion or behaviors, and is it shifting a largely collectivist, patriarchal society into something a little different?

International media generally continues to characterize Kuwait as a conservatively Islamic society and state still heavily affected by the 1990-1 Invasion, and while these are still very much true, Kuwait's society has continued to develop and change drastically in the last 30 years, and its young people engage with influences as diverse as local tradition and popular social media trends, as embedded in their own society as much as they are increasingly connected to the world beyond. The authors of our compiled articles each in turn present unique aspects of young people in Kuwait, which we hope can collectively present a more multi-dimensional cross-section of young people in Kuwait today. At the very least, it is our hope that these studies will help generate open, introspective conversations, helping us critically question and understand the way the youth and young adults in Kuwait – and beyond – experience and navigate themselves and the world around them.

Media Habits in Kuwait

Media consumption in Kuwait has evolved over the years starting with its advent and rise of radio and TV channels, to the rapidly-growing digital sphere and instant access to diverse media due to technological advancement as well. Media as a term is loosely used encompassing the different means of communication, the message itself and the effects it propagates to its audience. The Kuwait media system is more akin to European and North American models than those of other developing countries due largely to security measures for modernization in communications following the Gulf War.

Kuwait's oil-based wealth has empowered the state to invest in modern communications networks to serve its populace. This proliferation of media technology means that Kuwaitis, and the large population of expatriates living in Kuwait, have access to competing viewpoints than those of state-run television and media as well as those of more traditional channels like radio or printed newspapers. With foreign satellite television showing American and British TV shows and movies, an influx of commercially distributed and black-market Hollywood DVDs and CDs in the 2000's, and now streaming media, increasingly Kuwaitis are seeking out mediated messages and images that are not homegrown.

Kuwait has some of the most liberal media laws in the Persian Gulf and all of the Middle East. The Kuwaiti constitution guarantees freedom of the press and freedom of expression, as long as disrespectful statements targeting Islam and disrespectful or libelous statements about His Highness the Emir of Kuwait and the Crown Prince are avoided. More than 78.3% of the Kuwaiti population report listening to the radio and 46% watch TV regularly. With Kuwait having close to an 80% literacy rate, local newspapers, overwhelmingly in Arabic, still are the dominate source of information in the country despite widespread access to the Internet and foreign satellite television. Most of Kuwait's TV and radio-broadcast news have been historically fed through the Kuwait News Agency (KUNA), the national wire and a branch of the Ministry of Information. KUNA also provides significant local news content to newspapers like Press Reference and Reporters Without Borders. In 2006, Kuwait liberalized its publication laws, opened its doors to new newspapers and radio and TV broadcasting stations.

The local media and its content creation is usually tailored to fit cultural parameters, influenced largely by what its audiences deem acceptable and worth consumption. However, many youth and young adults consume Western media messages: growing exposure and possibilities of connecting to other communities, globalization has created the bridge of various ideologies through media. Foreign content started to become intertwined with the local ones and has become increasingly socially acceptable as well, particularly since the exposure to such content is also coupled with personal access and experiences through travels and overseas education by individuals. TV has been a prominent medium of information and entertainment for people in Kuwait, and continues to be a route for consumer-focused brands to further connect with their customers through commercials. Also, in seasons such as the holy month of Ramadan, where filmmaking and TV shows become an integral part of the family routine, the prominence for TV as a medium continued to grow.

In today's digital age, on-demand content has also become readily accessible with streaming services such as Netflix, Shahid TV and Hulu. Additionally, the recent surge and interest in foreign (especially Turkish and Indian-language) drama, young people's exposure to more culturally diverse content continues to influences their perceptions. The young people in Kuwait, especially Kuwaiti youth, largely consume Western media, including film TV, and social media. As a result of the modernization of communications, young adults have grown up in a media system that is very different from those of their parents.

The constant consumption of this media and introduction and saturation of Western media have contributed to the construction of the social identities, and when it comes to relationship building. Identities are also developed differently on a digital level. Due to the limitations enforced by the culture in terms of social interactions outside of family, Kuwait's population could become prone to behaving differently when interacting digitally, and with the opposite sex, by deviating from the norms if they were to interact face-to-face, within socially-acceptable parameters.

More than 90% of Kuwait's population use the internet (Kemp, 2022). Many consume web technology in methods that reinforce local traditions, such as spreading Islam but with so much foreign discourse available online, there are still real fears. More than 30 percent of university students surveyed said that they regularly used the Internet to breakdown traditional cultural dating folkways by meeting up with the opposite gender. "Internet in Kuwait is leading to experimentation, especially among youths, which could lead, sometime in the future, to the interruption of Kuwaiti traditions" (Wheeler 2000, p. 442).

This accessibility of social media influences the individual's social identity as it allows them more space to interact with others and also be selective of the type of content they prefer to engage with. Users have also become the content creators themselves with the increasing rise of social media channels such as TikTok and other platforms, which allows the individuals to create and express their own identity and share it with the world. Social media influencers play a huge role in socialization, identity formation, and consumer behavior, as platforms such as Instagram and SnapChat have given rise to Kuwaiti-based social media celebrities, many of whom have followers in excess of 2 to 3 million people. Many of the social media influencers tend to extend liberal views on fashion, socializing, and gender roles, which often results in lively national dialogues.

CHAPTER 2

Social Learning

GIVEN THE COLLECTIVIST nature of the Kuwaiti society, there are certain expectations from the individuals enforced throughout their upbringing that they have to conform to, especially within their extended family circle. Those expectations are also influenced through social learning where the individuals observe their parents and elders of the families engaging in certain acts and it's implied that they will follow into their footsteps. Additionally, these individuals will want to act similarly to seek acceptance from their family and social circle. The individual's moral compass is influenced towards notions of altruism and giving emphasis to the society as a whole, compared to oneself. When looking closer at this phenomenon and considering gender differences, which are also deeply rooted into this society, we come to notice that males are foreseen and believed to be more altruistic. Given the nature of the conservative society in Kuwait which implicitly discourages women, constantly while growing up, that they are not permitted or allowed to interact outside the realm of their home, in where they are expected to be the primary source of help and support. Due to gender segregation in the society as a whole and it being practiced across many of its sectors, including workplace as well, males are more likely to be offering help to strangers on the road compared to females, because the males are the ones who are mostly allowed to be made available to support. Also, due to societal practices, and religious beliefs which also play a vital role, males are expected to provide assistance to others, if and even if weren't asked. A sense of social obligation and duty shadows over the males more than the females and is enforced through social learning and inherited societal practices. The frequent observing of certain social acts, ideologies, especially when exhibited by close family members such as the parents, build up a series of behavioral expectation that both males and females seamlessly grow to follow and pass on to generations to come. Starting with the university phase, which is considered the first stage for youth's social interaction and their first out-of-home experience to enforce their personal identity, youth begin to interact with various social circles while embracing their social identity. The way this identity is shaped and evolved is continually affected during this phase. Individuals as university students are subtly pressured by the nature of this educational environment where expectations by their professors are different compared to high school. Students are expected to engage, interact and bring their ideas forward. In its infancy, their identities could be either fragile or intimidating, and the peer pressure or fear of being judged by others is always in the back of their heads, influencing how those identities continue to form. Kuwait's schooling system is gender segregated, and universities continue to adopt a similar module where applicable. One of the main new social experiences, for most students, who received their education in governmental schools, subsided by the government, is the interaction with the opposite sex. This social interaction greatly affects and shapes the individual's identity, role in the society, and expectation of the opposite sex, whether as a partner or social coexistence. University life is the first step into the real world, where individuals start to shine over a group. Strong and solid personal skills would aid the individuals in attaining prominent and prestigious statuses in the society, which would generally require a certain level of interaction with counterparts, possibly of the opposite sex, which they may not be socially equipped for. In a social sphere where males and females are mutually exclusive, yet a digital sphere provides the opportunity for both sexes to interact online, they may continue to lack certain skills or behavioral cues, which they might have intuitively acquired during direct interaction if permitted. This social barrier will continue to exist and influence the individual's identity, given the conservative nature of the society they live in and social expectations from family members, whose opinions and remarks greatly influence identities. Both males and females then continue to pursue their unique social identities, detached from the other gender, claiming superiority, which may then come to clash when they are bonded on a social level, and during marriage. The various societal expectations and opinions also affect how individuals react to uncommon practices such as expressing feelings and talking about mental wellness and possible illnesses associated. For example, depression in Kuwait hasn't been regarded as a serious mental health concern that is openly discussed between family members. Inhibiting such discussions instill the notion that individuals aren't allowed to suffer from related illnesses, which discourages any realization of the symptoms when noticed by others. Similarly, individuals who may be experiencing any negative thoughts would not feel safe to share how they feel, in fear of being judged by their family and having their identity questioned, especially in a collectivist society such as Kuwait's. The following section sheds light on the prevalent differences between males and females and how does a society such as Kuwait's contributes to those difference and enforces a clear and divided pathway for their social identity building, within the society. The psychological impact of practiced gender segregation is also examined to understand the effects this has on the forming of the youths' social identities. The case of depression is looked at closely, especially at the university level, where youth could be going through some challenges during this critical phase of their identity building and realization.

As published in the Journal of Education and Social Research –Volume 2, Issue 6, 2012– Page 97-104.

Altruism and Social Learning in Kuwait; an analysis of gender differences

Juliet Dinkha, Psy. D.
Charles Mitchell, M. Sc.
James Rose, Ph. D.
Tasneem Rashwan
Monica Matta
American University of Kuwait

Abstract

Our paper aims to identify the gender differences in helping behavior. It also seeks to explore how gender roles and prescribed norms affect the kind of helping behavior displayed by men and women in Kuwait, a collectivist society. In addition, we examine how altruism is related to the social learning theory and the effects of media as a major component of social learning. Authors explored whether altruistic behavior is impacted by observing others perform helping behavior. The Rushton et al. "Self-Report Altruism" scale was used to gather this information. We distributed 652 surveys to respondents between the ages of 18-33 living in Kuwait. The main findings were concluded that males living in Kuwait are more altruistic than females and as both males and females get older, they tend to help more. Furthermore, the results show that there is a strong correlation between the social theory and altruistic behaviors. In Kuwait, both culture and religion emphasize that men are expected to provide help both at home and work, whereas women are only expected to provide help at home.

Keywords: Altruism, Social Learning Theory, Gender, Media, Collectivist Society

Altruism

Being kind to others and outwardly performing acts of kindness is universally considered to be ethical. Whether one chooses to perform an act of kindness; however, is contingent on many variables: the nature of the relationship, need for help, and sense of responsibility to help the beneficiary amongst other factors (Meissner, 2003). A set of criteria can be used to define altruism:

"Altruistic behavior (a) must benefit another person, (b) must be performed voluntarily, (c) must be performed intentionally, (d) the benefit must be the goal by itself, and (e) must be performed without expecting any external reward" (Piliavin & Charng, 1990, p. 30).

Still, many others disagree. Some theorize that there is no true sense of altruism, that any act of kindness can inevitably be traced back to self-interest and the satisfying one's own ego. These two divergent views are framing modern inquiry into the study of altruism. According to Emmerik and Jawahar (2005), helping behaviors are "activities entailing more commitment than spontaneous assistance in which time is given freely to benefit another person, group, organization or cause" (p. 347). There are two types of helping behaviors. The first type is helping that happens within one's own group such as friends, relatives and close neighbors, also called organizational citizenship behaviors (OCBs).

"Helping behaviors differ on two dimensions, the familiarity with recipient and moral obligation." (p. 349)

In other words, an individual would filter out whom they would help, inclining more towards people to whom they connect with or to whom they feel a true need for assistance. It is also common to volunteer for a cause that affects personally affects the individual rather than something they know nothing about. For example, a recovering alcoholic is more empathetic towards someone going through the same situation and is more likely to volunteer as a sponsor to help with problems he experienced earlier. Similarly, a parent would be keener to help a relative or a friend when a situation related to child rearing arises.

Still, despite a vast landscape of inquiry into altruism in the fields of psychology and sociology, scholars have struggled with the best empirical and methodological approaches to study the subject. The field of inquiry now has moved away from merely a philosophical debate to one that centers upon the origins of altruism. One of the challenges is trying to understand if altruism is merely a character trait that is learnt behavior or a genetic predisposition hard wired into one's genetic code (Losco, 1996; Meissner, 2003). Inherent forms of altruism are generally classified as *autonomous* altruism and *normative* altruism is based on social learning and conformity (Skarin & Moely, 1976).

Scholars subscribing to the autonomous paradigm posit that altruism is linked not only to evolutionary traits but also to human nature. The idea being that one can be as concerned with others as individuals are concerned with themselves, underscoring a strong human propensity for compassion (Meissner, 2003). One point of view on the derivation of altruism is rooted in the Judeo-Christian idea of the Golden Rule, which states that one should love others as one loves oneself (Meissner, 2003). But this idea of being a Good Samaritan is still grounded in the tenets of the social learning theory, as these religious ideas need to be transmitted through social religious settings such as attending church or through Bible study classes.

Several studies have found that altruistic expression was less about being a Good Samaritan but was often times linked to amends for wrongdoing (reparative altruism). This approach routinely aligns altruism with guilt and adherence to social norms frequently involving trial and success until optimal or acceptable altruistic behavior was adopted. To this end, investigations have found that altruism can at times rise out of private situations outside of group or public displays, leading some to wonder how much of altruism as social learning is in fact conformity to group norms (Losco, 1996). Conversely, the limit here is perhaps a lack of understanding that social learning may be at work outside of group situations once it has been adopted. For example, one may choose to eat with a knife and fork, and with a napkin placed in their lap, even though they are eating home alone, when adhering to proper etiquette can be precluded altogether outside a group dining setting.

Another challenge is that individual differences need to be factored in any time an experiment is conducted into altruism. Many studies emphasize external forces and often times mitigate the individual differences of subjects in the experiments (Losco, 1996). Still, despite these individual differences studies show that altruistic tendencies and behavior increases as we age (Meissner, 2003).

Altruism, Age and Gender

Research findings suggest that just other factors change and develop as children age, so too does the understanding and expression of altruism. Many of these variables are linked to cognitive development and the constant assessment of child's own judgment of morality. So the expression of altruism will become stronger as a child grows and cements moral judgments. Data however doesn't just place the construction of altruism solely on cognitive development; it further stresses that there is a compounding effect of both cognitive development and socialization processes on altruism (Skarin & Moely, 1976; Losco, 1996). As the child grows and develops higher cognitive function they rely on models upon which to base their actions.

"As children grow up, their altruism may be increased because of growing empathic sensitivity, greater ability in perspective-taking, broader knowledge of cultural norms, increased social responsibility and competence, or enhanced moral reasoning capabilities." (Piliavin & Charng, 1990, p. 38)

Males are socialized to be competitive and assertive, while female are socialized to be caring, subservient and dependent. Females conform with the role of care provider who fulfills a function which is contradictory to the male role. Some studies propose females may be socialized to be more in tune to the emotions of others more so than men are (Eisenberg & Strayer, 1987; Skarin & Moely, 1976).

In a sample of 11 studies on gender and empathy, the results were comparable across the collection of data. What the research showed was that females consistently scored higher on the empathy scale (Eisenberg & Strayer, 1987).

In a field experiment conducted on children ranging from ages 5 to 12, the females in the trial demonstrated the highest levels of altruism. The significance of the findings signify that females are conditioned to be caregivers and so are more likely to help other children needing help and males are socialized to be competitive so are less likely to assist. The only noted exception being females were less likely to help out if the altruistic act was one of physical aid directed toward the males, as this was seen as inconsistent with the female gender role (Skarin & Moely, 1976).

Piliavin & Unger (1985) found different results: Looking at a sample of adults, their data indicated that men and women were equally likely to engage in altruistic behavior. The only difference noted is that women would most likely engage in altruism in low-level scenarios in addition to high-level; whereas men generally only acted in high-level scenarios. This disparity again was attributed to gender roles where females reported more often providing emotional support and counseling to friends, while men tended to indicate only lending aid when the action was more high risk or protection was needed (Piliavin & Charng, 1990). Still, overall, women in the literature were more likely to engage in altruistic behavior than men.

Social Learning Theory

Baldwin et al. (2004) contends that the social learning theory is behavior that one learns from observing those around them. This observation however is not limited to personal interaction and routinely includes mediated messages from both television and movies. Albert Bandura first developed the theory in the 1960's. He proposed that both adults and children learn through the process of observation (Baldwin, 2004; DeFleur, 2004).

The paradigm emphasizes that media acts upon individuals. Adults and children learn acceptable behavior through consumption of these media messages. Therefore behavior is not only learnt or modeled but rather it is adopted (Baldwin, 2004).

The theory was initially applied to the subject of learnt violent behavior and subsequently extrapolated from aggression to other types of learnt behavior. Bandura posits that in a social setting behavior was learnt and adopted by simply watching others and seeing their behavior as positive (DeFleur, 2010). By observing or by consuming mass media, the social learning theory would conclude that trial and error could be circumvented, and through observation and then adoption of appropriate behavior, one assimilates positive social behaviors. Social learning then could be constructed on a myriad of behaviors from how to dress, how to speak, how to act and suitable gender behavior for both male and females (Severin, 2001).

Bandura attempted to demonstrate the media effect of leaned violent behavior with an experiment on children. In the pioneering experiment, the Stanford University psychologist placed preschool children in a room and made them observe a video of adults hitting a plastic blow-up clown— Bobo; while another group of children watched the clowned being hugged. The children were then placed into the room with Bobo shortly after viewing the video. The kids then modeled the behavior demonstrated in the video: The ones who had seen the violent video began hitting the doll in a similar manner to the mediated message. Furthermore, the children elevated the violent behavior by picking up toys strewn throughout the room and hitting the doll with these other instruments in a manner more severe than what was demonstrated in the video. Conversely, the kids who viewed the video of the clown being hugged also duplicated the behavior they had observed (Dominick, 2009; Rubinstein, 1978; Baldwin, 2004).

An interesting twist in the area of social learning theory is how much of social learning is actually conformity. Nicolas Claidière and Andrew Whiten (2012) studied conformity and its relationship with social learning. Conformity is defined as that "behavior (that) is said to conform when an individual in a group displays behavior because it is the most frequent the individual witnessed in others." (p. 129) Looking at an experiment by Solomon Asch in 1955, Claidière and Whiten found that often times in experiments, respondents are unwilling to voice a dissenting opinion in a group setting even when they know they are right. Once they learn what behavior is appropriate they are routinely unwilling to diverge from this action.

The social learning theory is then much more than just learning through observation of friends, peers and media, but many individuals are conforming to group norms because they do not see their action or behavior as an individual choice. While social learning is mainly about acquiring new knowledge and demonstrating this through action, often times conformity is illustrating action that we have already learnt is appropriate. For example, if altruistic behaviors were acquired through social learning, then conformity would require an individual to demonstrate such behavior when the situation requires helping action. Several factors are listed as necessary for the conformity to occur: An individual

> "(a) has to choose between several alternative behaviors, (b) chooses the one displayed by a majority of other individuals, and (c) does so because it is the option chosen by the majority and not for alternative reasons." (p. 128)

In 1984, a researcher at Kuwait University replicated Asch's original study using cards and a group of actors (confederates), whose role was to mislead deliberately respondents by providing erroneous answers, in order to judge group influence on responses. The aim of the Kuwaiti experiment was to see if there would be a strong tendency for Kuwaiti undergraduates to conform to group norms and to see how conformity in Kuwait would rank compared to previous experiments conducted in other cultures. Many other studies had found little conformity (Amir, 1984) with many investigators concluding that the culture must play a heavy hand in conformity. For example, Asch's original experiment took place during McCarthyism, where conformity to group norms was especially high; and so effectively many subsequent experiments, didn't find the same effects Asch did. However, the recent Kuwait experiment was different. When the experiment was replicated here, results found that Kuwaiti students had a powerful propensity toward conformity. The results were comparable to the original Asch study in 1950's USA. This study reinforced several researchers claim that Kuwait's cultural makeup plays a strong role in conformity to group norms (Amir, 1984) and avoiding alternative chooses. We can surmise then that social learning is a strong force in the culture of Kuwait for acquiring norms such as altruism.

Gender in Kuwait

The interplay between family, tradition, and religion plays an important role in defining gender role. In Kuwait, males and females act in a certain way in order to gain acceptance in the society. Gender roles in Kuwait do not "only indicate specific roles for men and women to adopt, but also shape cultural and religious beliefs that structure men's and women's rights, access to resources, and mobility in society" (Torstrick & Faier, 2009, p. 112).

With respect to altruism, it's the norm that males will usually display altruistic behavior towards strangers, in addition to family members. "Men are expected to provide for the family and make major household decisions as well as those pertaining to children" (Torstrick & Faier 2009, p. 112). Their role is to stop and assist a person with a flat tire, or a person being attacked on the street. If a man doesn't assist the family, or in some cases the entire household, financially he is viewed as irresponsible. In Kuwait, families usually live in the husband's family house with extended family members (Torstrick & Faier, 2009) and the males are expected to provide financial aid for relatives in need. Conversely, females are most likely to display altruistic behavior with family members or in an indoor situation. For example, if a woman doesn't help with the household, this is considered disrespectful to the family and she will be stigmatized. In Kuwait, women are perceived as "weak...and that women's virtue must be protected." (Torstrick & Faier, 2009, p. 112). Thus the differences in the ways males and females are raised and treated within society defines the ways both will display altruistic behavior within that society.

In this paper we will be focusing on hypothesize the following:

1. Men will exhibit helping behavior more than women.
2. A female will less likely offer help to a male.
3. Helping behaviors increase with age.
4. Gender roles will determine the type of help offered by the individual

Methodology

We conducted our research by distributing the Self-Report Altruism questionnaire equally between both genders. The Self-Report Altruism Questionnaire is consisted of 20-items designed to examine the different types of altruistic behavior (Rushton, Chrisjohn, & Fekken, 1981). Participants were asked to rate the recurrence of their altruistic behavior using the categories 'Never', 'Once', 'More than Once', 'Often', and 'Very Often'.

In this study, we randomly selected the respondents with equal numbers of males and females in our sample. The questionnaire was given to a group of university students who were trained and supervised by the research team. The survey was distributed to ages 18-33. Many were distributed in universities, companies, and shopping malls.

Results

A total of 652 adults completed the Self-Report Altruism Scale. The sample size by age and gender is depicted in Table 1.

Age	Male	Female	Total
18-22	101	122	223
22-25	117	101	218
26-29	61	52	113
30-33	50	48	98
Total	329	323	652

Table 1. Final sample size by age and gender.

The Self-Report Altruism Scale yields scores ranging from 20 to 100. These scores were analyzed using a 4 x 2 factorial analysis of variance with age (18-22, 22-25, 26-29, and 30-33) and gender (male, female) as between-subjects factors. As anticipated, this analysis found a significant effect of age on these a scores, $F(3, 644) = 8.18$, $p<001$; a significant effect of gender, $F(1, 644) = 5.3$, $p<.05$; and no interaction, $F(3, 644) = .35$, $p=n.s.$ These results are depicted in Figure 1.

As illustrated in Fig.1, age was a defining variable in respondents' disposition toward performing altruism acts. There was a marked increase in the altruism scale scores from those 18 to 21 to those who identified as 30 to 33. While there wasn't a strong surge between each age group, the growth on the altruism scale increases incrementally with each higher age category. The results show a consistent increase on the scale, with the age of the respondents in our sample, demonstrating a substantial correlation with age and altruism.

Furthermore, when examined by gender our findings indicate that males tended to score higher on the altruism scale than females. This phenomenon was consistent and was observed in all age groups across our sample. Males in all age categories outscored females in the self-reported altruism scale, with the most marked difference observed with males and females 18 to 21. Given the lack of data specific to culture in our research, we can only hypothesize that perhaps as the students enter university stringent attitudes toward gender roles within the culture are broken down with each successive university year and exposure to academic ideas and classmates outside their usual socialization routes. However, given the limited amount of university students in older categories in our sample (98) we would need balanced sample sizes across age categories to draw stronger rationales for the disparity in gender.

Nevertheless, none of this diminishes the overall trends, which cogently demonstrate that no matter the variables, males of any age group are reporting higher levels of altruistic behavior and attitudes than females. n summary, our findings prove that males in our sample tend to gravitate toward altruism more so than females and that older subjects are more likely to score higher on the altruism scale than those who are 18 to 21, remaining consistent with our original hypothesis.

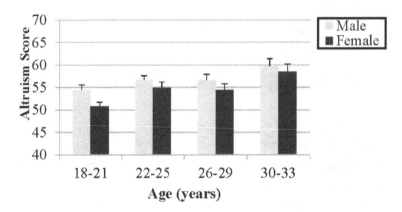

Figure 1. Mean (+S.E.M.) altruism scores by age and gender.

Discussion and Results

As predicted, males in our sample were more altruistic than the female respondents. These results are contrary to the data found in western countries where numerous studies have shown that females tend to have a higher propensity toward acts of selflessness than males (Eisenberg & Strayer, 1997; Piliavin & Charng, 1990; Skarin & Moely, 1976). In those investigations, it was reported that women are socialized to be primary caregivers in western societies and this conditioning translates to acts of altruism because of the social desirability in those cultures for women to be primary helpers (Skarin and Moely, 1976). This is generally true in the Kuwait as well, where women are the primary caregivers and men are the primary breadwinners (Torstrick & Faier, 2009). However, due to Kuwait being a more conservative society that does not allow women to help outside the realm of their home and extended family, we see a strong tendency for males to engage in more altruistic behaviors, especially outside of the home and with strangers. This would be especially true since the survey items were tailored to reflect altruism tendencies in the west by asking questions such as: "I have given a stranger a lift in my car" and "I have made change for a stranger." The behavior displayed in the situations presented in the survey questions would be considered taboo for females in a conservative Middle Eastern society.

In our research however, we found that social desirability toward altruism is culturally directed toward men. Due to the strict traditional gender roles and gender segregation women are not often expected to come to a person's aid outside of the immediate household. Men on the other hand, are conditioned through social learning processes to be engaging in altruistic behavior. As discussed previously, Kuwait is a patriarchal society where men are expected to be the breadwinners and to be the ones who have to help extended family members (Torstrick & Faier, 2009). This duty is largely attributed to the collectivist nature of Kuwait, where aiding others is part of the sense of obligation to traditional values and norms. For example, a man may be willing to stop and help a stranger with flat tire on the street while it is inappropriate for a woman to do the same. Similarly, a woman's duty may include helping in the home but it's not generally expected that she aid outside the home as her husband would. It's more acceptable for a man to offer aid outside of his familial role. By contrast, in western society, women often aid outside of their homes because their role as care provider often translates outside of the household (Eisenberg & Strayer, 1997; Skarin and Moely, 1976). However, our data demonstrates that this luxury only extends to the men in Kuwait. Moreover, the collectivist culture dictates that males are often mandated to live up to reputational, societal, and familial expectations. As a result of these factors, we deduce that these strict gender roles are what account for the disparity in Arab females' altruistic behavior compared to their western counterparts in our sample, and higher reporting of altruism behavior among the men.

Another result we found is that both males and females become more altruistic as they grow older. This is consistent with findings of similar studies conducted in the west. We believe that the reasons behind this are the same examples provided by Piliavin & Charng: as children grow older, they learn expected behavior from their parents, peers and media. These agents of socialization act are in accordance with the social learning theory, which says societal forces conditions both males and females to their roles in society (Baldwin, 2004; DeFleur, 2010). While one school of the altruism says that perhaps helping behavior is inherent, the differences between females in our study and those in western studies would refute this idea (Skarin & Moely, 1976). However, in line with the innate argument for altruism, we see an increase in levels of altruistic behavior as age and social experiences increase and gender roles and cognitive maturity crystallizes. Perhaps with age also comes an increase in cognitive abilities and a person rationalizes their behavior to offer aid (Skarin and Moely, 1976; Losco, 1976).

Even though some of the rigidity of Kuwait's culture is slowly being diluted with the effect of globalization and Western media imperialism, Kuwait is still a fairly conservative society that abides by rules and regulations set by the social learning: education, culture, family, religion and media. Males are continuing to see their roles as the primary helpers in and out of the home, with the existing social learning process, it seems unlikely that we will observe any decaying of this role in the foreseeable future.

Limitations and Future Research

The study had, or lacked, information that might have affected our results, such as the survey makeup. The survey was more western centric; in other words, the questions that were asked focused on what a western women would do, such as offering a stranger a ride. However, females in Kuwait, feel it's often times inappropriate to offer physical aid to strangers. Another theory is perhaps social learning of religious traditions says women should limit their interactions with strange men, so perhaps males are helping both genders and women are reporting less helping behavior because they are helping other women primarily. The gender of those being helped would have to be measured. A follow-up investigation would have to be initiated to determine why women and men help and why they don't help, to understand the social learning processes that encourage or discourage people in Kuwait from altruistic behavior. Moreover, variables such as media, parents and peers could be examined independently to gauge the contribution of each agent on altruistic behavior.

References

Amir, T. (1984). The Asch conformity effect: A study in Kuwait. *Social Behavior and Personality, 12*(2), pp. 187-190.

Baldwin, R. J., Perry, D. S., & Moffitt, A. M. (2004). *Communication Theories for Everyday Life*. Illinois State University. Person Education, Inc.

Central Intelligence Agency. (2012). The World Factbook: Kuwait. Retrieved February 8, 2012.

Çetin, M. "Voluntary Altruistic Action: Its Symbolic Challenge against Sinecures of Vested Interests" (paper presented at the second annual "Islam in the Contemporary World: *The Fethullah Gülen Movement in Thought and Practice"* conference, Norman, Okla., Nov. 3-5, 2006), 1-21.

Claidière, N., & Whiten, A. (2012). Integrating the study of conformity and culture in humans and nonhuman animals. *Psychological Bulletin, 138*(1), 126-145. doi: 10.1037/a0025868

Dakhli, M., Dinkha, J., & Matta, M. (2010). Educational attainment and career success in the GCC: does gender matter? *AUK Occasional Papers. 4.*

DeFleur, M. L. (2010). *Mass communication theories: explaining origins, processes, and effects.* Boston: Allyn & Bacon.

Dominick, J.R. (2009). *The dynamics of mass communication: media in the digital age.* Boston: McGraw-Hill Higher Education.

Eisenberg, N. & Strayer, J. (1987). *Empathy and its development.* (2nd ed.). Retrieved from Google Books on 16 November 2011.

Emmerik H. V. & Jawahar I. M. (2005). Lending a helping hand: Provision of helping behaviors beyond professional career responsibilities. *Career Development International, 10*(5), pp. 347-358.

Felson, R. B. (1996). Mass media effects on violent behavior. *Annual Review of Sociology, 22*, pp. 103-128.

Losco, J. (1986). Understanding altruism: A critique and proposal for integrating various approaches. Political Psychology, 7(2), 323–346.

Meissner, W. W. (2003). *The ethical dimension of psychoanalysis: the dialogue*. Retrieved from Google Books on 16 November 2011.

Mikulincer, M., & Shaver, P. R. (2005). Attachment security, compassion, and altruism. *Current Directions in Psychological Science, 14*(1), pp. 34-38.

Neusner, J. & Chilton, B. (eds.). (2005). *Altruism in world religions*. Retrieved from Google Books on 16 November 2011.

Piliavin, J. A., & Charng, H. (1990). Altruism: A review of recent theory and research. *Annual Review of Sociology, 16*, pp. 27-65.

Piliavin, J. A. & Unger, R. K. (1985). The helpful but helpless female: Myth or reality? *Women, gender, and Social Psychology*. Hillsdale: N. J.: Erlbaum.

Press References. Kuwait. Retrieved from http://www.pressreference.com/Gu-Ku/Kuwait.html

Reporters Without Borders (2010). Kuwait. Retrieved from http://en.rsf.org/report-kuwait,156.html

Reporters Without Borders (2010, January). Kuwait. Retrieved from http://en.rsf.org/kuwait-kuwait-05-01-2010,35449.html

Rubinstein, E. A. (1978). Television and the young viewer: The pervasive social influence of television on children is being increasingly documented, but has yet to be translated into a continuing and effective social policy. *American Scientist, 66*(6), pp. 685-693.

Rushton, J. P., Chrisjohn, R. D., & Fekken, G. C. (1981). The altruistic personality and the self-report altruism scale. Personality and Individual Differences, 2(4), 293-302. doi: 10.1016/0191-8869(81)90084-2

Skarin, K., & Moely, B. E. (1976). Altruistic behavior: An analysis of age and sex differences. *Child Development, 47*(4), pp. 1159-1165.

Severin, W. J., & Tankard, J. W. (2001). *Communication Theories: Origins, Methods, and Uses in the Mass Media*. New York, NY: Addison Wesley Longman.

Torstrick, R. L., & Faier, E. (2009). Gender, marriage, and family. In *Culture and customs of the Arab Gulf States* (p. 112). Westport, CT: Greenwood Press.

Wheeler, D. (2000). New media, globalization and Kuwaiti national identity. *Middle East Journal, 54*(3, The Information Revolution), pp. 432-444.

As published in the Journal of Psychology and Education –Volume 47, Issues 1&2, 2010– Pages 23-24.

Psychological Impact of Gender Segregation

Dr. Juliet Dinkha
Sarah Mobasher
Nour El-Shamsy
The American University of Kuwait (AUK)

This study explores the rationale behind educational gender segregation and its psychological outcomes. An online survey conducted by the Student Government Association (SGA) aimed at understanding if gender separation was manifested as the result of religious or cultural views and what psychological effects it is going to have on present and future interaction between the sexes. The results were interpreted using Albert Ellis' model of Cognitive Rational-Emotive Therapy and were correlated to a 2006 SGA study that was issued in response to the Kuwait law imposing gender segregation in private universities.

Keywords: Gender Segregation, Psychology, University, Kuwait, Cognitive Therapy

Introduction

The idea of gender segregation is very controversial. In developed countries it is seen as a violation of human rights. In the Gulf region it is a social process that is becoming massively enforced even within private universities whose origins stem from highly developed countries. The perception among the sexes in the developed countries is that men and women are more similar than different (Williams & Best, 1989). The countries in the Arabian Gulf are some of the most prominent countries that enforce gender segregation in public and private education. Eleanor Abdullah Doumato, a specialist in gender and history of the Gulf region, explains that religion is the reason preventing coeducational schools in the Middle East. She states that living in Saudi Arabia demonstrates to her how eager their society is to create segregation between males and females (Doumato, 2002). Saudi Arabia is not the only country that promotes and enforces gender segregation. Kuwait passed two laws that imposed gender segregation in which the state's public system was to be segregated in 1996, which was implemented in 2001. The second law followed in 2000 and has yet to be fully implemented (Al-Khaled, 2008).

According Lolwa Al Qattami, Chairwoman of the Women's Cultural and Social Society, Kuwait is a democratic country, not an Islamic one. "Other Muslim countries allow integration of male and female students in schools and universities. Does this mean these countries base their laws on Islamic principles different from what we follow in Kuwait?" Islam does not impose segregation of the sexes but regulates integration of men and women (Roberts, 2008). This is supported by the Quran, "O mankind! We have created you from a male and a female, and made you nations and tribes, that you may know one another..." (Quran 49:13). It is expected then for Muslims to know one another, be they male or female. This is logical, with socialization comes understanding and interconnectedness. Understanding and interconnectedness brings concern and compassion for the well being one for another. Protection and care then becomes societal and not just the obligation of a single family or a single man. With segregation the familiarity caused by socialization will be lost, therefore those benefits that come with it will be lost. Noura Al-Ghanem, owner of the Universal American School, said the owners of British, American and bilingual schools created, and have obtained approval, not only from the local authorities but from the international institutions as well to provide education to both genders and doing otherwise will only raise doubts on their credibility (Roberts, 2008).

Literature Review

In 2007 the research of Dr. Giedd showed there was "no overlap in the trajectories of the brain development of boy and girls" (Giedd, 2007). This indicated the different regions of the brain develop in a different sequence in girls compared to that of boys. This was utilized to claim separate classes should be offered as a tool for the separate genders to excel (Single-sex classes, n.d.). However, not all the facts agree. The divisions of the brain in both males and females begin to develop in the third week or embryonic stage of gestation (*Gray's Anatomy*, 1977, p1279). According to the anatomical development shown human males and females form in the same way neurologically. The neurons are not connected at birth; through life experiences these connections are created, strengthened, or pruned away (Blair, 2002; Huttenlocher & Dabholkar, 1997; *Gray's Anatomy*, 1977). Furthermore, the strength of these connections is what causes humans to remember (Blair 2002; Huttenlocher et.al., 1997). What a child experiences then can strengthen or prune away used or unused connections, indicating children are malleable (Blair 2002; Lewis, 1997). The study of Brown (2004) showed single-sex public schools produce higher grades and test scores, based on the belief that students in segregated schools do not feel challenged by the opposite sex and do not feel the need to attract the opposite sex and therefore concentrate on their studies. Not every expert agrees. In some parts of the world, whether students attend segregated or non-segregated schools has no impact on their academic success and personalities in the long run. Alan Smithers, a professor of education at Buckingham University, explains that although ten percent of the schools in Hong Kong are single sex schools and that girls get the best results, in Belgium, where the majority of schools are segregated, it is the co-educational schools which have the best results. Smithers clarifies that the advantages of segregated schools are exaggerated (Asthana, 2006).

The laterality differences of the brain as shown by I.Q. testing, brain mapping with Computed Tomography, and Magnetic Resonance Imaging are utilized in giving rationale for segregation of sexes. Research shows boys are right brain dominant and are recognized for their scholastic achievements in math and visual spatial recognition. Girls, according to such research, are left brain dominant and excel in verbal skills, such as reading and writing ("Gender Differences Impact Learning and Post-School Success," n.d.). These studies would indicate segregated school would aid students to learn at their own pace and help their brain develop according to their gender differences; that such classes give students freedom to act unrestricted in class at all times. When students reach puberty, these researchers explain, it is important to allow each gender to freely experience this crucial phase naturally without having to endure the burdens of the opposite sex teasing them("Gender Differences," n.d.). However, others contend, and the growing consensus in gender research is, the differences between sexes have been exaggerated (Hyde &Plant, 1995). Beliefs that males are dominant, independent, aggressive, achievement oriented and enduring while females are believed to be nurturing, more social, less esteemed and more helpful in distress are stereotypical (Williams et. al. 1982). Crawford and Unger (2000) showed as children grow they develop gender roles due to expectations of how a male and female should think, act, and behave. Hyde and Plant (1995) cited only in gifted populations do males outperform females in math. Linn and Peterson (1986) showed females were not always lacking in visual spatial tasks; the inability to rotate objects in the mind were the only consistent difference. The stereotyping of a female being more nurturing than a male was disproved by Whiting in 1989. This study validated that the cultures in which children of both sexes equally assist in the care of younger siblings result in the same nurturing behaviors. Harassment and teasing behavior were studied by Rachel Simmons. Her book *Odd Girl Out: The Hidden Culture of Aggression in Girls* (2003) features case studies showing girl-on-girl teasing and harassment are both common and harmful; the assumption that removing the boys from school will automatically remove the aggressors is in itself based on a stereotype.

The negative psychological effects of gender segregation on higher education are noticeable in the psychological impact on students. In non-segregated institutions, educational leaders approach educational policy and practice by allowing students to work things out interactively and not to intervene too closely in students' interactions. The college and university perform as agents of socialization, and the administration and faculty recognize students bring with them when they enter the university different identities that have been shaped by their parents, their communities, and their religions. These differences in students help their growth and development in the university

(Hurtado, Milem, Clayton-Pederston, & Allen, 1998). In the most recent studies conducted by the National Association for Single Sex Public Education, it appears that co-educational schools had an adverse effect on participants; these schools reinforce gender stereotypes rather than diminishing them. However, recall the words of Chief Justice Earl Warren while delivering his decision in the famous case of Brown versus the Board of Education: "We conclude that, in the field of public education, the doctrine of 'separate but equal' has no place. Separate educational facilities are inherently unequal." Herding female students into separate schools would make it much easier to deny them funds, supplies, and course materials that would allow them to compete with their male counterparts.

Segregation in the school may well lead to future segregation in the work place. A part of the reason for the remarkable persistence of gender segregation over time is that it is intimately linked to sexist attitudes. Carol Vogler (Scott, 1994) cited males engage in sex typing to protect their privilege and harassment is used to prevent female intrusion into their occupations. She also stated these attitudes may not only play an important role in legitimatizing and stabilizing segregation in the labor market, but also may inhibit the possibility of shifts to desegregation (Scott, 1994). Ethnologist James Taggart stated, "Gender segregation is an important dimension of gender relations because, as cross cultural research reveals, gender segregation is necessary although not a sufficient condition for sexual hierarchy" (Taggart, 1992). The practice of occupational gender segregation has been accepted as a form of gender inequality. High levels of segregation are considered to be a significant factor in the discrepancy between the wages of women and men, imposing constraints on careers, and generally to be at the root of gender inequalities (Blackburn & Jarman, 1997). Research as early as 1944 showed men experienced "status contradictions" when working with females as equals; gender equality at work potentially threatened the other patriarchal social structures that benefit them (Hughes, 1944). As a result, men possess an interest in segregation at work that reflects their desires to preserve dominance in the larger society (Sokoloff, 1980). Patterns of gender segregation are sustained by tradition as much as by rational strategies of individual employers and employees

(Connolly & Townshend-Smith, 2004). "Behavior that brings physical and psychological gains is notoriously easy to rationalize as being not only justified but quite logical, natural and perhaps even righteous" (Coleman, 1976).

THE STUDY

Methodology

The sequence of the study was conducted in this order. First, the review of the 2006 study on gender segregation and then review the results of the 2008 study we conducted using the Albert Ellis Cognitive Rational Emotive Therapy model.

Comparison Study

The 2006 study was conducted by the Student Government Association (SGA) of the American University of Kuwait (AUK) in response to the Kuwaiti parliament passing a law that imposed gender segregation on private universities in Kuwait; 525 students participated in the survey: 248 were female and 277 were male. Both groups consisted of numerous students with different nationalities. They were asked to identify themselves as Kuwaitis or non-Kuwaitis. Of the females, 190 were Kuwaitis and 58 were non-Kuwaitis; of the males, 204 were Kuwaitis and 73 were non-Kuwaitis. The survey was distributed by hand to fill out and give back to the S.G.A. There were fourteen questions that dealt with gender segregation. Out of these fourteen, six questions were selected as relevant for comparisons to this survey. The six questions were as follows: 1) co-educational classrooms violate Islamic beliefs; 2) co-educational classrooms violate Kuwaiti moral values; 3) co-educational classrooms improve communication between people of opposite genders; 4) co-educational classrooms help to prepare students for mixed-gender employment environments; 5) segregated classrooms hinder the learning process; and 6) the partition placed between male and female students in AUK classrooms inhibits the learning environment. The results of this study were then placed in the Albert Ellis Cognitive Rational Emotive Behavior Model.

The Model

Albert Ellis (1913-2007), considered the father of the Cognitive Emotive Rational Theory of behavior and acclaimed for the ABC model representative of human thoughts and feelings, defined his model as A being representative of external environmental events, B being representative of cognition, and C being representative of the resulting action or emotion displayed. His theory demonstrates how beliefs about an event can help to determine the response and therefore the outcome. If beliefs are rational they lead to moderate emotions that allow people to act constructively. On the other hand, irrational beliefs can lead to dysfunctional emotions such as anger, anxiety, or depression, which stop people from achieving their goals (Opre & Opre, 2006).

According to Ellis, humans experience activating events (A) every day that prompt them to think about what is occurring. The interpretation of these events results in specific beliefs (B) about the event and the individual's role in the events. Once the belief is developed, the emotional consequence (C) is experienced based on the belief (B). An example of this would be a student is placed in a co-educational classroom. This would be the activating event (A). The student might believe that co-education is wrong and it defies his moral and cultural values. This would be the cognition or thought occurring (B). The consequence of this is the student will feel uncomfortable in the co-educational classroom and acts in an irrational manner. This would be the experience (C) based on the belief.

This model is used to explain the results from the survey and their implications on the students and society in general. The model fits well with the exception of the activating event (A) which does not cause the belief (B) but instead is the trigger for a belief already present. This, of course, produces the consequence (C) evident in the results of the survey. The underlying cause of the segregation debate in Kuwait, as well as other Islamic countries, is the teaching that gender integration is wrong, or somehow un-Islamic. The interpretation of the activating event is based on a belief already present. If the event correlates positively (congruence) with the interpretation, then the response will be positive. If the event correlates negatively (contradicts), then the emotion response is negative.

The Study

This study was conducted in response to the discussion of the law that imposed gender segregation in private universities. The segregation law triggered a response among the students of those universities. The Student Governmental Association (SGA.) conducted the survey with the researchers choosing the student body of the American University of Kuwait (AUK) as test subjects. These students have experienced the benefit of co-educational classrooms at the university level, thereby making them optimal for this research. At first, the survey was divided into Kuwaiti and non-Kuwaiti nationalities, however this yielded no significant differences between these groups. Therefore, the groups were combined for the purpose of this research.

Due to the sensitive nature and possible repercussions of participation in such a study the students were asked to complete the survey online at their discretion. The total number of participants was 867. The survey consisted of the following nine questions:

Q1: What type of classroom do you feel best supports learning?

1. Fully segregated - separate classrooms for each gender
2. Partially segregated genders - separated by use of dividers
3. Coeducational - fully mixed gender classrooms
4. No preference

Q2: What type of environment do you prefer for common areas on campus (i.e. library, seating areas, eating areas, coffee shops, etc.)?

1. Fully segregated - separate space for each gender
2. Partially Segregated - genders separated by use of dividers
3. Coeducational - fully mixed gender common areas
4. No preference

Q3: How do you feel that fully segregated classrooms will impact the quality of your education?

1. Improve the quality of my education
2. Lower the quality of my education
3. Have no effect
4. No opinion

Q4: How do you feel that a fully segregated campus environment will impact your social skills?

1. Improve the development of my social skills
2. Restrict the development of my social skills
3. Have no effect
4. No opinion

Q5: What type of environment do you prefer for university student activities/events?

1. Fully segregated - separate activity/event for each gender
2. Partially Segregated - genders separated by use of dividers
3. Coeducational - fully mixed activities/events
4. No preference

Q6: How do you feel that a fully segregated campus environment will impact interaction between the genders in the workplace?

1. Improve interaction in the workplace
2. Lower interaction in the workplace
3. Have no effect
4. No opinion

Q7: Should a person residing in Kuwait be given the option to choose from a coeducational (mixed) educational environment or a segregated educational environment?

1. Yes
2. No
3. No opinion

Q 8: Would you be willing to participate in activities if they were fully segregated (i.e. clubs, organizations, and trips)?

1. Yes
2. No
3. Yes, but I prefer mixed activities
4. No opinion

Q9: If Kuwait were to be a fully segregated society, how will this affect its relationship with other countries?

1. Have a positive affect
2. Have a negative affect
3. Have no affect

Results and Discussion

The results obtained from the 2006 survey indicated 52% of the male group agreed co-educational classrooms violate Islamic belief, 55% of the female group disagreed; 57% of the male group agreed co-education violates Kuwaiti moral values, while 55% of the females disagreed.

Sixty percent of the male group believed co-educational classrooms do not improve communication between people of opposite genders, while 58% of the females believed co-educational classrooms improve communication between people of opposite genders.

In the male group, 62% believed co-educational classrooms do not help prepare students for mixed gender employment, while 60% of the female group believed co-educational classrooms help prepare students for mixed gender employment; 49% of the male group believed segregated classrooms do not hinder the learning process, while 44% in the female group agreed segregated classrooms hinder the learning process.

Forty-five percent of the males believed the partitions placed between male and female students in AUK classrooms do not inhibit the learning environment, while 47% of the female group believed the partitions placed between male and female students in AUK classrooms inhibit the learning process.

The results obtained from the 2008 survey indicated 78.8% of students voted for coeducational classrooms as the type of classroom that best supports learning; 90% of the students preferred a coeducational environment on campus (seating areas, eating areas, etc.); 62.6% of students felt fully segregated classrooms will impact the quality of their education; 83.7% felt a fully segregated campus would restrict the development of their social skills; 84.4% of the students preferred a coeducational environment for university student activities and events; 85.5% of the students felt a fully segregated campus environment will lower interaction between the genders in the workplace. Of those students who participated, 85.6% voted yes for people in Kuwait to be given the option to choose from a coeducational environment or a segregated educational environment.

Forty-one percent of students voted yes for participating in segregated activities but preferred mixed activities; 88% of students stated that if Kuwait was to become a completely segregated society this will have a negative effect on its relationship with other countries.

The 2006 survey highlighted the gender differences present among students in AUK in regards to gender segregation. According to the results, several conclusions can be drawn as to what male and female students think about gender segregation. Males, as is evident from the results, are oriented towards gender segregation for several reasons. They regard co-education as a violation of Islamic beliefs and a violation of Kuwaiti moral values. Although gender segregation is embedded within the Kuwaiti culture and value system, it is not a violation of Islamic beliefs. Islam regulates gender integration but does not forbid it (Al Fadli, 2008). Males in this survey also believed co-education does not improve communication between the sexes and that it does not prepare students for mixed-gender employment. They feel gender segregation does not hinder the learning process and the partitions placed between male and female students do not inhibit their ability to learn.

These beliefs are indicative of Albert Ellis' *ABC Model* "based on the assumption emotional problems come from a dysfunctional thinking style about certain events and not the events themselves" (p. 42). Males are supportive of gender segregation because the *Activating Event* (A) is male and female together in class, *Belief* (B) is co-education is wrong. Emotional or behavioral *Consequences* (C) is to feel uncomfortable in co-educational classes, hence the support for gender segregation.

Another interpretation, as previously evidenced, is male employment in a mixed or female-dominated work setting (whether it is in a job or university) may threaten men's masculine identities and lower their perceived self-esteem and well-being (Wharton & Baron, 1987). Therefore, the majority of male students were in favor of gender segregation. This can be tied to what Sokoloff stated, as cited earlier in this paper; that working with females as equals, and gender equality at work, threaten other patriarchal social structures and therefore men possessing an interest in segregation at work reflect their desires to preserve dominance in the larger society (Sokoloff, 1980).

Females are very supportive of co-education and regard gender segregation as a means that hinders the learning process and inhibits it. A possible interpretation is that women have long been oppressed and denied their rights to a proper education. Previously, it was prohibited for a female to work. Today females are being trained, welcomed, and introduced into the occupational world. Women are competing with men in the workforce and are working to equate their rights. Women feel co-educational classrooms help prepare them for mixed-gender employment and help improve their communication with the opposite sex. This is regarded as a beneficial tool to aid them in their newly granted right to work.

In the 2008 survey, results indicated the majority of the students were in favor of co-education. They feel it not only supports their learning process, but gender segregation will have an impact on the quality of their education and social skills and will have a negative effect on Kuwait's relationship with other countries. Using Ellis' model, it can be surmised (A) students placed in segregated classrooms; (B) feel is detrimental to their present learning and future social processes and (C) will create anxiety, anger and depression which are not conducive to learning.

Conclusion

Gender segregation has been in the Arabian Gulf for many years. Much research has been done in support of segregation all over the world, yet gender segregation is only now becoming a serious issue. Nations are growing, and through continued research and development are becoming more aware of the impact different factors have on a society, such as gender segregation. Only through positive educational experience of the youth can a society have general well-being.

Gender segregation in the Gulf is being adopted for reasons with which children and young adults of the next generation disagree. Females are more often opposed to segregation than males, mainly because *males will benefit from segregation and maintain superiority over females*. Though some have purported gender segregation has been effective in terms of schooling, the opposing research shows its detriment. It has also been shown to be detrimental in social and racial issues, as well as in breaking gender stereotypes and creating a sense of community in society.

Limitation and implication for future research

Due to the lack of data on gender segregation in the Gulf, it has been difficult to gather adequate data for this research. In addition, the sample representatives were insufficient. A larger more substantial sample is required to clearly show the effect of gender segregation on students. Since surveys were not translated, this could have limited the number of participants or could have altered the results, due to misunderstanding of the questions. Furthermore, future research should look at other schools in the Arabian Gulf region and try to compare the results to this research to get a broader look at the issue of segregation in the entire region.

References

Al-Fadli, N. (Mar. 2008). The Great Divide. *The Voice of AUK.*

Al-Khalid, A., (Feb. 2008). Segregation Law wasteful. *Arab Times.*

Asthana, A. (Jun. 2006). Single-sex schools 'no benefit for girls'. Retrieved January 16, 2008, from Education Guardian Web site HYPERLINK "http://education.guardian.co.uk/schools/story/0,,1805641,00.html"

Blackburn R.M., & Jarman, J. (1997). Occupational Gender Segregation. *Sociology at Survey Unis*, 16.

Blair, C. (2002). School Readiness: Integrating Cognition and Emotion in a Neurobiological Conceptualization of Children's Functioning at School Entry. *American Psychologist*, 57, 111-127.

Brown, E., (2004). Gender segregation serves schools well. Retrieved Feb. 2008 from website http://www.thebatt.com/

Crawford, M. & Unger, R., (2000). *Women and Gender (2nd Ed.)*. New York. McGraw Hill.

Coleman, James C. (1976). *Abnormal Psychology and Modern Life (5th Ed.)*. Glenview. Scott, Foresman and Company.

Connolly, M. (2004). *Townshend-Smith On Discrimination Law: Text, Cases and Materials* (2nd Ed.). London:Cavendish.

Doumato, E. (2002). Separate and unequal: Sex segregation in a Saudi national obsession. Retrieved January 5, 2008, from Brown University News Service Web site: HYPERLINK "http://www.brown.edu/Administration/News_Bureau/2001-02/01-110.html"

Gender differences impact learning and post—school success. Retrieved January 2, 2008, *Council for Exceptional Children*: http://www.cec.sped.org/

Giedd, J. (2007). Sexual dimorphism of brain developmental trajectories during childhood and adolescence. *NeuroImage*, 36(4), 165-173.

Hughes, E. 1944. Dilemmas and Contradictions of Status. *American Journal of Sociology*, 50:353-59.

Hurtado, S., Clayton-Pedersen, A., & Allen,W., (1998). Enhancing Campus Climates for Racial/Ethnic Diversity: Educational Policy and Practice. *The Review of Higher Education*, 21.3, 279-302.

Huttenlocher, PR. & Dabholkar, A.S, (1997). Regional Differences in Synaptogenesis in Human Cerebral Cortex. *Journal of Comparative Neurology*, 37(2), 167-178.

Hyde, J.S., & Plant E.A., (1995) Magnitude of Psychological Gender Differences: Another Side of the Story. *American Psychologist*, 50, 159-161.

Grays Anatomy. 1977. New York. Crown Publications, Inc.

Lewis, M. (1997). *Altering Fate: Why the Past does not Predict the Future*, New York. Guilford Press.

Linn, M.C. & Peterson, A.C. (1986). A meta-analysis of gender differences in spatial ability: Implications for mathematics and science achievement. In H.S. Hyde & M.C. Linn (Eds.). The psychology of gender: Advances through meta analysis. Baltimore. *The John Hopkins University Press*.

Opre, A., & Opre, D. (2006). The Gender Stereotype Threat and the Academic Performance of Women's University Teaching Staff. *American Sociological Review* Vol. 52. No.5

Roberts L., (14 Feb. 2008). College segregation a waste of money. *Arab Times*.

Scott A. M., (1994) *Gender Segregation and Social Change: Men and Women in Changing.* London: OUP Oxford.

Simmons, Rachel (2003). *Odd Girl Out: the Hidden culture of Aggression in Girls.* Fort Washington, PA. Harvest Books, LLC.

Single-sex education. Retrieved January 2, 2008, from *NASSPE: National Association for Single Sex Public Education*: HYPERLINK "http://www.singlesexschools.org" http://www.singlesexschools.org

Sokoloff, N. J. (1980). *Between Money and Love.* New York: Praeger.

Taggart, J, N. (1992). *Gender segregation and cultural constructions of sexuality in two Hispanic societies.* USA: Springer.

The Rise and Fall of Jim Crow. Jim Crow Stories. Brown v. Board of Education. PBS. Retrieved March 12, 2009. HYPERLINK "http//www.pbs.org/wnet/jimcrow/stories_events_brown.html

Wharton A. S., & Baron J. N. (1987). *So Happy Together? The Impact of Gender Segregatino on Men at Work.* American Sociological Review, 22(1), 48-72.

Whiting, B.B., (1989, April). Culture and interpersonal behavior. Paper presented at the biennial meeting of the *Society for Research in Child Development,* Kansas City.

Williams, M.F., & Best D.L. (1982). *Measuring Stereotypes: A Thirty Nation Study,* Newbury Park, CA. Sage Publication.

As published in the Journal of Psychology and Education –Volume 49, Issues 1&2, 2012– Pages 7-18.

The Risk of Depression and Suicide Among University Students of Kuwait: A Cross-Study of Three Universities

Dr. Juliet Dinkha & Sarah Mobasher
American University of Kuwait (AUK)

Depression and Suicide risk was studied in students of three leading universities of Kuwait, The American University of Kuwait (AUK), Gulf University for Science and Technology (GUST), and Australian College of Kuwait (ACK). Participants told in advance they would be required to fill out a BDI-II and a questionnaire formulated to gain data on students understanding of depression and suicide. Data from the questionnaire was subjective; therefore, only common words or themes expressed were considered and recorded. The remaining responses were place in a category of other. The result was that although depression was more significant in the participants of the study, the knowledge of depression and even the acceptance of depression existing in Kuwait was limited.

Keywords: Depression, Suicide, University, Social Acceptance, Social Support

Introduction

On February 14, 1978, Sheikh Jaber Al-Ahmad, Amir of Kuwait, said "the Kuwait of tomorrow belongs to the Kuwaiti youth, men and women alike. The country is surging forward to a bright future based on the confidence, will, and determination of its youth." To the Kuwaiti government, these were not just words. This oil rich nation used its wealth to elevate its people with social welfare projects. Among other benefits, these projects decreased infant mortality through health programs, increased material possessions with subsidies, and improved learning with an expansive educational system.

In 1990, Iraq invaded Kuwait. The children of Kuwait who had lived all their lives in peace and prosperity were now the witnesses to war. With bombs dropping and fellow citizens being gunned down in the streets, the adults were pre-occupied with finding food and shelter for their families. The security and abundance these children had never questioned was replaced with fear and a struggle to just survive. Torture was common during the occupation and atrocities occurred daily in public view. Kuwait was liberated in 1991, but the seeds of trauma had already been planted deep within these children. Today these same children are the students of higher education in Kuwait. The Kuwaiti society is relatively conservative and freedom of expression of certain feelings, including depression, is looked on in a disparaging manner.

Literature Review

This trauma, along with societal and educational issues, can easily lead to depression. Depression is the most widely known psychiatric disorder, with its history being as old as the study of psychiatry itself (Sham& Hand, 1993). Historically, it was believed that children lacked the maturity to become depressed (Rie, 1996). This belief has been dismissed; research has made it evident depression can occur at any age. It manifests in differing symptoms that can occur in early childhood, through adolescence, and into adulthood (Perry-Jones, 1989).

Armsworth and Holaday (1993) cites the effect of trauma, such as war or the loss of a loved one, is both horrendous and is difficult to estimate, and children who experience it have an increased tendency to develop depression. In Kuwait, many children have family members who were martyred in the war, or were held prisoner. Caruso (2005), while studying the trauma of rape, states the emotional, physical and mental pain can easily trigger severe depressive episodes leading to suicide. Studies show that children who are depressed are more likely to develop episodes of depression as adults (Moore& Carr 2000). For the depressed child, working through adolescence may be complicated by depressive symptoms such as weight gain and feelings of worthlessness (DSM-IV).

The expectation is that adolescents may experience stressors related to body image and social acceptance, but a severe difference from what is considered "normal" can also lead to societal rejection and depression. Studies of clinical samples of children who seek treatment for obesity seem to support there is also an association between depression and obesity (Britz, 2000; Erermis, 2004). Children associate obesity with several undesirable traits (Staffieri, 1967; Hill, 1995) and prefer to associate themselves with average weight peers (Richardson, 1961; Turnbull, 2000). Overweight children are more likely to become victims of bullying than other children, (Janssen, 2004) . The bullied child or adolescent frequently experiences feelings of shame and ridicule in social interaction, which in other circumstances would not be socially tolerated (Scheff, 1988). Logically, the bullied child (especially the bullied child already depressed due to trauma), will experience a deepening of depression and a worsening of symptoms. Moore and Carr (2000) have shown that children with depression have more depressive episodes than adults.

This, too, is true for children who experience racism. Not all children of Kuwait are Kuwaiti; as Kuwait was historically a less developed country, and its location on the Arabian gulf made it perfect for fishing and a port for the import and export of goods, tribal leaders and merchant families accumulated wealth through commerce with the British (Lawson, 1985). Societal class structure evolved from these original clans (Lawson, 1985). According to Lawson (1985), two thirds of these families made up the cabinet and one third made up the directorships of shareholding companies in the 1960's and 1970's; this ruling coalition was reinforced fifteen years later after Kuwaiti independence. The Kuwaiti ruling class structured the society, creating high-paying jobs for all Kuwaiti nationals unable to find employment in the public sectors (Lawson, 1985). This elevated the standards of living of Kuwaiti nationals in society. However, when oil revenues began to pour into Kuwait after the Second World War, creating vacancies for workers to support the new industry, migrant workers began to fill this void. By 1997, these foreign workers outnumbered the Kuwaiti workers two to one (Kuwait Census, 1997). A law in 1995 allowed the sponsoring of maids, which contributed to this increase, and also to the stereotyping of immigrants as domestic help and manual laborers. This lead to social, economic, and political discrimination against them in the form of suspicion, if not outright hostility (Shah & Al-Qudsi, 1986).

While studying the relations of perceived racism and externalizing symptoms, Nyborg and Curry (2003) found that there is a correlation between racism and depressive symptoms. They noted children who are subjects of perceived racism had a decreased self-concept, a higher sense of helplessness, and an increase of depressive symptoms. Such research indicates that depression in expatriates' children may be aggravated by the added stress of racism. According to the National Institute of Mental Health in the United States, the highest rates of suicide are in minority groups who have to deal with racism on a daily basis (NIMH, 2004). The University of Kuwait reports that non-Kuwaiti students have surpassed the numbers of Kuwaiti students with females in higher numbers than males (Al-Eberheem & Stevens, 1980).

Cultural influences of religion, family, and prior schooling structure must also be considered when studying depression in Kuwait's students of higher education. Islam is the dominate faith in Kuwait, and it plays an important role in daily life (El-Alami & Hinchcliffe, 1999). The norms and rules of the religion are seen as very important (Dinkha & Dakhili, 2008). A Muslim is asked to self evaluate his or her deeds according certain Islamic principles and guidelines. These guidelines must be strictly observed. Failure to do so is disobedience to the Islamic bindings, which causes great shame and can force the individual to withdraw from society. Suicide, and the depression leading to it, is in conflict with the ideology of Islam and is taboo in Moslem life and culture. The soul is viewed as a precious entity owned by God; therefore, humans have no right to interfere by killing this soul. This inhibits the Muslim from even expressing thoughts of suicide (Inter-Islam, 2007).

This societal stigma is so strong, Kuwaiti media will sometimes attempt to outright deny suicide and suicide attempts even happen, especially if the victim is a Kuwaiti national. Sabah El Salem (1/3/2007) reported a Kuwaiti girl attempted suicide by ingesting disinfectant, but the family insisted it was an accident; this is a common claim for not only family, but the media itself, to make. Suicides and suicide attempts made by foreign laborers and domestic help are reported more often, but the stigma is still there. The Al Rai Daily (2008) reported an Egyptian woman admitted to Adan Hospital was being charged for a case of attempted suicide for attempting to take her life by overdose of medication. Meleis (1982) found Arab students in Western Universities deal with mental state instability by claiming it to be a physical complaint; they neglected their anxiety and depression, and substituted it with a somatic complaint, since mostly everyone experiences illness. Only after repeated visits were physicians able to identify the need for a psychologist. When depression is recognized by Kuwaiti medical personnel, they do offer treatment, but clients prefer medication to psychotherapy because they fear someone might see them regularly attend appointments. The client may also discontinue treatment for fear it will appear in their medical history.

The source of depression can also be much closer to home. Familial structures in Kuwait encourage younger members to rely on their elders for guidance (Meleis, 1982). Relatives and close family members assist in decision making, showing how much they care for the younger. Meleis (1982) said that Arab students and families recognize that education is a vital ingredient for improvement and modernization. As a result, families in Kuwait seek more professional education systems. The choice of the major is predetermined by the parents and grade point average. High academic standards are placed on the student by the family; the student is expected to maintain his family's social class. The United States statics (2005) states suicide, due to social pressure, is the second leading cause of death for college students. Parental rejection and parental control can lead to self-criticism and indecisiveness, both symptoms of depression (Furr, Westfeld, McConnell, & Jerkins, 2001). Brown and Harris (1978) cited parental rejection contributes to self-denigration, which increases the risk of depression. Because of the severe social stigma associated with suicide and suicidal thoughts, even when overwhelmed by self-criticalness, indecisiveness, and loss of pleasure, a student waits until they are unable to function before seek professional help, if they seek help at all.

The educational struggles themselves can result in depression. Furr, Westfeld, McConnell, and Jerkins (2001) found college students' reasons for depression, aside from parental pressure, were financial problems, academic problems, loneliness, and hopelessness. Some students did not even know why they were depressed. In Kuwait, there are six hundred and eight government schools and thirty nine private schools (Ministry of Education, 2008), and although Arabic is the official language of Kuwait and government schools teach in Arabic, private schools and University classes are taught near-exclusively in English (KU, 2007). Due to the ratio of government schools to private schools, most students entering University must adjust to classes being taught in English (Hamady, 1960). Students moving from government schools to a private based system have difficulties adapting to this change, which can add another burden.

Conceptual Framework

Eighteen years ago, Kuwait was liberated from Iraqi invaders. The students now in University were children during this war. College can be a difficult period where students may feel lost, lonely, confused, anxious, inadequate and stressed under the best of circumstances. Along with the normal social, academic, and family stressors that cause depression and suicide, the added stressor of the Iraqi war is manifesting in Kuwaiti University students today. Abdel-Khalek and Soliman (1999) showed, in a cross-cultural study, Kuwaiti children have a decreased depression mean score than their American and Egyptian counterparts; however, they also noted that age and culture interacted significantly to affect this decrease.

Hypothesis/Questions

The societal norms and Kuwaiti views on suicide, paired with the aftermath of war, have increased the prevalence of depression and suicidal thoughts in Kuwaiti College students. In spite of this increase, however, there is still a lack of understanding of depression and suicidal ideation among those at risk.

Questions

To explore this hypothesis we considered these two questions: what is the prevalence of depression and suicidal thoughts in Kuwaiti Universities, and how is that depression experienced and recognized among students in Kuwait attending Universities?

Method

Subjects

It was difficult to find students willing to fill out the BDI-II and suicide questionnaire. Some cited a false belief that depression and suicide did not exist in Kuwait. Three hundred eighteen students were surveyed from three universities. The gender distribution was 42.2% males, 48.1% female, and 9.5% unreported. The students were all attendees of The American University of Kuwait (AUK), The Gulf University for Science and Technology (GUST), or the Australian College of Kuwait (ACK). The AUK is a co-educational liberal arts institution of higher education. The GUST offers four year degrees in science and business administration and ACK offers a two year degree in business administration and engineering. AUK is the only one of these universities that has classes related to suicide (AUK, 2008).

Apparatus and Procedure

The Becks depression inventory two (BDI-II) was utilized to measure the students' depression levels and a suicide questionnaire adapted for the Kuwait culture was also distributed to the same test sample. The BDI-II is an independent questionnaire rating twenty-one items indicative of the symptoms of depression. The students were asked to circle the statement that best described the way they were feeling in the last two weeks. The questionnaire was subjective and focused on the students' idea of how suicide is expressed and perceived in Kuwait. The students were asked to write down their responses to these four questions. How serious is a person claiming he/she will commit suicide? What are the common verbal expressions that indicate suicide rates in Kuwait? What are the various methods used to commit suicide in Kuwait? What course of action should be taken if someone is expected to commit suicide?

The BDI-II and the suicide questionnaire were randomly distributed to the students at AUK, GUST, AND ACK with an accumulated sample of three hundred and eighteen participants. The BDI-II was scored and analyzed. The results of depression were calculated accumulatively for all the universities. The suicide questionnaire was examined for common words and themes. All answers were kept confidential and were coded using a number system. Students' identities were kept anonymous.

Results

The results complied for the BDI-II showed that 10% of the students were severely depressed, 14% were moderately depressed, 19% were mildly depressed and 56% were in the minimal rage. In addition to the prevalence of depression, the factors contributing to these results were ranked in a descending order according to the BDI -II scores. The symptoms most seen in the sample were the following: crying 29.56%, self criticalness 21.70%, loss of pleasure 17.61%, indecisiveness 16.98%, tiredness and fatigue 16.35%, punishment feelings 15.72%, difficulty concentrating 15.40%, agitation 15.40%, pessimism 13.84%, and feelings of guilt 13.52% (Table 1).

The suicide questionnaire that examined the participant's general knowledge of suicide found these common themes and words. In question one regarding seriousness of a person claiming he/she will commit suicide? The student answered they could tell by the 'Tone and way of speech,' 'sadness and depression,' 'I don't know,' 'facial expression,' 'other,' 'negative view of self and world,' and 'loss of faith' (Table 2).

On question two, the responses reported when inquired about common verbal expression that indicate suicide in Kuwait were as follows; 'it isn't talked about or expressed,' 'I don't know or blank,' indirect claim of "I'm going to kill myself' and 'I hate life, and I feel depressed' (Table 3).

In question three, various methods used to commit suicide were listed: jumping off a building, overdose on medication, car accidents due to speeding, knives or any sharp objects, hanging, guns, and poisoning (Table 4).

The final question four addressed the course of action that should be taken if someone is believed to be suicidal. Participants noted that they would advise the other, talk to him/her, tell them not to do it. Other answers were call the police, get help from elders through negotiation, I don't know, and seek professional help (Table 5).

Of the obtained results, focus was placed on finding credible answers to each of the three questioned addressed in this study. The first question related to the prevalence of depression and suicide. Al-Otaibi, Al-Weqayyan, Taher, Sarkhou, Gloom, Assen, Al-Mousa, Al-Zoubi, and Habeeba (2007) in their study regarding ill patients of primary health care facilities found only 7.0% had severe depression and 13.5% were moderately depressed. These university students, while in the robustness of their youth, scored 24% reflecting moderate to severe depression among the participants. The most reported symptoms were crying, self criticalness, loss of pleasure, and indecisiveness.

In the knowledge of depression questionnaire, the Kuwaiti students recognized crying 29.5% as the most common expression of depression. Self-criticalness was listed second while loss of pleasure and indecisiveness ranked third and fourth consecutively. Students 43% said they would offer personal help to prevent a person from committing suicide compared to the 14% that said they would seek professional help.

Discussion

In 1994, three years after liberation, Asem (1994) showed 16.8% of Kuwaiti children had Post Traumatic Stress Disorder. Many of these children are the university students of today. The stress of these older teens and young adults of Kuwait to fulfill the traditional cultural standards while meeting modern expectations while carrying the crippling emotional scars of war is apparent. Social class, religion, family, academic stressors and language barriers are added burdens of the students of Kuwaiti Universities. This research shows that the students in university today are at greater risk than the general population for depression and the end result of untreated depression, suicide. It further shows that while at a greater risk for depression the students have a decreased ability to deal with it due to the lack of understanding of depression and suicide. The universities, while offering the skills need to advance the careers of these students, are not meeting their proven psycho-social needs. Depression and suicide education as a mandatory part of the educational process would assist in remedying the current as well as future needs of the entire culture.

Education of these students in depression and suicide will give understanding in what is depression and how to recognize and handle suicidal remarks made by peers. Suicide Awareness Voice of Education (SAVE) show appropriate steps that decrease suicide numbers: 1) converse with them and convince them to get professional help 2) don't keep it a secret; seek professional help 3) don't try to minimize the problem or shame the person into changing their minds 4) offer to work cooperatively with a psychologist (SAVE, 2003).

As studies dealing with depression and suicide are limited in Kuwait, this research is intended to be a beginning for future work in how the children who experienced the trauma of war cope with the remaining stressors that are now present and await them in the future. Understanding any obstacle is the first step in removing it from the path of success. If the existence of the obstacle is denied, it cannot be removed. Education is critical in removing it from the students of today, and since those students will grow and become the elders sought for advice, it is the key in preventing it in the students of tomorrow. There is a social and religious stigma now applied to a suicidal person that can only be erased with recognition, understanding, and education. The goal is, of course, to help the sufferer and overcome the disease, bringing them a satisfying and successful life.

References

Abdul-Khalek, A.M., & Soliman, H.H. (1999). A cross-cultural evaluation of depression in children in Egypt, Kuwait, and The United States. *Psychological Reports, 85,* 973-980.

Al- Najjar, A. (2006, December 12).Asian attempts suicide. *Al Wattan* newspaper, p. 18, American Foundation for Suicide Prevention, (2008). When You Fear Someone May Take Their Own Life. Retrieved from http://www.afsp.org/index.cfm

Al-Otaibi, B., Al-Weqayyan, T.H., Sarkhou E., Gloom A., F. Aseen, Almousa E., Al-Zoubi H., & Habeeba S., (2007). Depressive Symptoms among Kuwaiti Population Attending Primary Healthcare Setting: Prevalence and Influence of Sociodemographic Factors. *Medical Principals and Practice, 16,* 384-388.

American University of Kuwait, (2008). Academics: Categories & Requirements. Retrieved from http://www.auk.edu.kw/default.jsp

An Egyptian woman attempts suicide. (2008, May 8). *Al Rai* daily newspaper Asem, (1994, Sept 11). Percentage of Children Affected with PTSD after the War. Al Rai, Al Al-Islam p.4.

El Alami & Hinchcliffe, Kuwait, *Civil Society,* vol. 8, issue 90 (June 1999): 10-11 Ghosh, Shuvo, Sexuality: Gender Identity: Jul 20, 2006.

Armsworth, M.W., & Holaday, M. (1993). An investigation into the observed sex differences in prevalence of unipolar depression. *Journal of Abnormal Psychology, 9.*

Beck, A.T. (1977). *Depression and suicide: Contemporary approaches to research and treatment.* In J. P. Brady, J. Mendels, M. T. Orne, & W. Rieger (Eds.), Psychiatry: Areas of promise and advancement (pp. 171-178). New York: Spectrum.

Borgquist, A. (1906). Crying. *The American Journal of Psychology*, 17, 149-203, Retrieved 7,14,2008, from http://www.jstor.org/stable/1412391

Britz B, Siegfried W, Ziegler A, et al. (2000). Rates of psychiatric disorders in a clinical study group of adolescents with extreme obesity and in obese adolescents ascertained via a population based study. *International Journal of Obesity Related Metabolic Disorders: Journal of the International Association for the Study of Obesity*, 24, 1707-1714.

Brown, G.W., & Harris, T.O. (1978). *Social Origins of Depression: A study of psychiatric disorder in women.* New York: Free Press

Canning, H., & Mayer, J. (1966.) Obesity—its possible effect on college acceptance. *New England Journal of Medicine*, 275,1172-1174

Caruso, K. (2005). *Depression and suicide.* Retrieved June 10, 2008, from http://suicide.org

Centers for Disease Control and Prevention (CDC) (1998). *Depression and Suicide.* Greenwood Press

Dinkha, J., & Dakhli, M (2008). *Perceived Discrimination in the Arabian Gulf: The Case of Migrant Labor in Kuwait.* Under Review.

Dinkha, J., & Abdulhamid, S. (2008). How identity is constructed in Kuwait: Analysis of four case studies. *Psychology Journal 5(4),* 190-211.

Dolgan, J. I. (1990) Depression in children. *Pediatric Annals,* 19, 45-50.

Erermis, S., Cetin, N., Tamarm M., Bukusoglu, N., Akdeniz, F., & Goksen, D. (2004). Is obesity a risk factor for psychopathology among adolescents? *Pediatrics International, 46,* 296-301.

Figueiredo, H. (2005). Gender and Depression. Society for Neuroscience 35th Annual Meeting, Washington, News release, University of Cincinnati.

Furr, S., Westefeld, J., McConnell, G., & Jerkins, J. (2001). Suicide and Depression Among College Students: A Decade Later. *Professional Psychology, Research and Practice, 32*(1) 97, Retrieved 7,18,2008.

Green, A. H. (1985). Children traumatized by physical abuse. In S. Eth & R. S. Pynoos (Eds.), *Post-Traumatic Stress Disorder in Children*. Washington, D.C: American Psychiatric Press, pp. 133-154.

Hamady, S. (1960). *Temperament and Character of the Arabs*. New York: Wayne Publisher.

Hil,l A.J., & Silver, E.K. (1995). Fat, friendless and unhealthy: 9-year old children's perception of body shape stereotypes. *International Journal of Obesity Related Metabolic Disorders: Journal of the International Association for the Study of Obesity, 19*, 423-430.

Inter-Islam, (2007). Joint Sahih-Bukhari Completion & Graduation. Retrieved July 19, 2008, from Suicide as seen in Islam Web site: "http://www.inter-islam.org/Prohibitions/suicide.html"

Janssen, I., Craig, W.M., Boyce, W.F., & Pickett, W. (2004). Associations between overweight and obesity with bullying behaviors in school-aged children. *Pediatrics, 113*,1187-1194.

Kuwait Information Retrieved July 18, 2008, from Ministry Of Education Web site: http://www.kuwait-info.com/sidepages/state_ministries_education.asp

Kuwait Ministry of Education, February 1989. Kuwait on the March. *Al-Arabi Magazine*, p.204.

Kuwait University, (2007). Academics and Research. Retrieved July 19, 2008, from Kuwait University Web site: "http://www.kuniv.edu.kw/"

Kuwaiti girl attempts suicide. (2007, March 19). *Kuwait Times*.

Kuwaiti lady attempts suicide by swallowing pills. (2007, March 1). *Kuwait Times.*

Kuwaiti woman jumps off and eleven storey apartment. (2007, March 18). *Kuwait Times.*

Meleis, A (1982).Social Properties and Dilemmas. *Arab Students in Western Universities. 53,* 439-447.

Malone, K, Haas, G, Sweeney, J, & Mann, J (1995). Major depression and the risk of attempted suicide. Elsevier Science B.V., Retrieved07,12,2008, from "http://www.sciencedirect.com/science"

Moore, M.,& Carr, A. (2000) Depression and grief . In A. Carr (Ed.), *What works with children and adolescents? A critical review of psychological interventions with children, adolescents and their families.* (7th ed.) New York: Routledge, Taylor & Francis. pp. 203-232.

National Institute of Mental Health, (2008,06,26). Retrieved July 12, 2008, from How is depression detected and treated? Website: "http://www.nimh.nih.gov/ health/publications/depression/treatment.shtml"

National Institute of Mental Health, (2004). Retrieved July 12, 2008, from Suicide in the U.S.: Statistics and Prevention Website: "http://www.nimh.nih.gov/health/ publications/suicide-"

Parry-Jones, W. L. (1989) Depression in adolescence. In K R. Herbst &E. S. Paykel (Eds.), *Depression: an integrative approach.* Oxford UK: Heinemann.

Richardson, S., Goodman, N., Hastorf, A.H., & Dornbuch, S.M. (1961). Cultural uniformity in reaction to physical disabilities. *American Social Review, 26,* 241-247.

Rie, H.E. (1966). Depression in childhood: a survey of some pertinent contributions. *Journal of the American Academy of Child Psychiatry, 5,* 653-685.

Scheff, T. (1988). Shame and conformity: the deference-emotion system. *American Social Review, 53,* 395-406.

Staffieri, J.R. (1967). A study of social stereotype of body image in children. *Journal Personality and Social Psychology, 7,* 101-104.

Suicide Prevention Resource Center, (2005). Suicide Prevention Basics. Retrieved July 19, 2008, from Suicide Prevention Web site: "http://www.sprc.org/"

Suicide Awareness Voices of Education. (2003). Suicide Prevention Information. Retrieved July 19, 2008, from Prevent Suicide. Treat Suicide Web site: "http://www.save.org/"

Thamer, A. (2006, December 11). Suicide in Fahaheel. *Al Qabas newspaper,* p. 25.

Turnbull, J.D., Heaslip, S., & McLeod, H.A. (2000). Pre-school children's attitudes to fat and normal male and female stimulus figures. *International Journal of Obesity Related Metabolic Disorders: Journal of the International Association for the Study of Obesity, 24,* 1705-1706.

Van Der Kolk, B. A. (Ed.) (1987). *Psychological trauma.* Washington, DC: American Psychiatric Press.

Appendix

Table 1. Symptoms of Depression in three private universities

Rank	Depression Symptoms	Overall Percent
1	Crying	29.56%
2	Self Criticalness	21.70%
3	Loss of Pleasure	17.61%
4	Indecisiveness	16.98%
5	Tiredness and Fatigue	16.35%
6	Punishment Feelings	15.72%
7	Concentration difficulty	15.40%
8	Agitation	15.40%
9	Pessimism	13.84%
10	Guilty Feelings	13.52%
11	Self- Dislike	13.52%
12	Loss of Interest	13.20%
13	Suicidal Thoughts or Wishes	11.95%
14	Loss of appetite	10.69%
15	Loss of Interest in sex	10.37%
16	Past Failure	9.43%
17	Worthlessness	9.11%
18	Irritability	8.80%
19	Loss Of Energy	7.54%
20	Change in Sleeping Pattern	7.23%
21	Sadness	6.92%

Table 2. Percentage Distribution of responses to: *How serious is a person when claiming that they will commit suicide?*

Rank	Percentage Distribution of Question 1	Overall Percent
1	Tone and Way of Speech	21%
2	Sadness and Depression	15%
3	I Don't Know	13%
4.5	Facial Expression	12%
4.5	Other	12%
5	Negative View of Self and World	10%
6	Loss of Faith	5%

Table 3. Percentage Distribution of responses to: *What are common verbal expressions that indicate suicide rates in Kuwait?*

Rank	Percentage Distribution of Question 2	Overall Percent
1	"It isn't talked about or expressed"	21%
2	"I don't know"	20%
3	directly said "I'm going to kill myself"	15%
4	indirectly said "I hate life, I feel depressed"	15%

Table 4. Percentage Distribution of responses to: *What are the various methods used to commit suicide in Kuwait?*

Rank	Percentage Distribution of Question 3	Overall Percent
1	Jumping off buildings, rooftops, high stories	30%
2	Overdose drugs including pills	27%
3	Speeding and car accidents	25%
4	Sharp Objects (Knives) and cutting wrists	21%
5	Hanging themselves	18%
6	Guns	11%
7	Poisoning	7%

Table 5. Percentage Distribution of responses to: *What course of action should be taken if someone is expected to commit suicide?*

Rank	Percentage Distribution of Question 4	Overall Percent
1	"Talk to him and advise him not to"	43%
2	" Call the police"	16%
3	"Other "	15%
4	" Seek adult and professional help"	14%
5	" Blank or Don't know"	13%

CHAPTER 3

Media Evolution

SIMILARLY TO HOW Social Learning is practiced and the individuals are influenced through observing their family members interact in a society, so has media perceptions crawled in and accumulated into the back of the individuals' brains influencing how they evaluate themselves and others. Subsequently, one cannot overlook the evident impacts of being exposed to media, both traditional media and emerging digital media, especially in today's world and amidst the rise of technological advancements. Media, as a term in our inquiries, refers to the various means of mass communication, accessed by the individual and the messages being carried. The level to which individuals are affected by media is also dependent on numerous other factors, and personality filters that vary between individuals. However, there is no doubt that the media role in the Kuwaiti society had evolved and progressed tremendously over the years, carrying western ideologies and characteristics that soon grew to be socially accepted as a norm by the majority of the society. As a result of this intertwining channeling of messages and content with the everyday life, the society has become more receptive and susceptible to being influenced by media content. Media, such as TV, is a reflection of the society since it is created by individuals who are from the mainstream social groups. Also, since media is a form of representation, there is a sense of freedom in what can be represented and the type of content created and disseminated, in accordance to each country's media law. Additionally, with technological advancement allowing a seamless access to different media sources, foreign channels and content, there is no limitation to what we can be exposed to, and influenced by. The limitless access media provides to the users allow them to dive deep into dissecting their image and appearance within a society seeking alternations to conform to and become more popular and accepted according to the new norms induced by the media. Additionally, the social media channels, such as Instagram, are offering the individuals the opportunity to express themselves, while also exploring their social identify and personality traits further, through the sharing of user-generated content. Since this content can be customized, edited, filtered, and limited to whom can have access to it, users can create and share the version of themselves they wish to share with others, whether it's a true reflection or not. Furthermore, as social identities continue to draw its threads and self-construct, and amidst the constant exposure to widely available media content, identities tend to find themselves at a cross path between imagined and true identities. Due to the nature of the Kuwaiti society, its culture and societal limitations on interactions outside the family, a majority of the individuals are susceptible to forming parasocial relationships with media personalities. This form of attachment is embraced with the swift access to media at our fingertips, which allows individuals to be in constant connection with their favorite TV characters. The individuals' social identities can then become influenced through this media attachment as they navigate a true identity. Thus, their expectations of real life relationships are skewed by their parasocial relationships. This form of attachment affects their overall social identity development and how this identity plays a role in the society in general. There are also evident differences and trends in media consumption through a gender lens. Such differences follow into the steps of the societal assumptions and expectation inherited by both genders, especially in a collectivist society as Kuwait. What men and women are allowed to consume of media and carry its effects into their everyday life is greatly dependent on their environment and how media has played a role in their social circle. Additionally, whether certain imitated behaviors influenced by the media are accepted or not is restricted socially for both men and women. Open access media provides individuals with a portal to a vast range of ideologies, concepts and behaviors, which are learned and imitated subtly. One's identity and principles could offer guidance on what to select from this content and what to discard. We cannot ignore the fact that media consumption actually begins at an early age and has a deep-rooted basis to how media is integrated in one's life and being consumed. Therefore, it's important to also consider the media role and impact in the lives of children, as this is the younger version of the social identity that is yet to be developed. The following section starts with examining the relationship between the child and the parent in correlation to media consumption, their viewing habits and social learnings, mainly of violent behaviors, and how is this influenced through media. The correlation is also observed in light of various factors that might be of significance to the parental controlling habits practiced. Additionally, since the effects of media imperialism in Kuwait are evident, we will be presenting how the individuals, and society subsequently, observe themselves when compared to media images and the reflection on their own body images, which are perceived negatively and with levels of dissatisfaction. This social comparison exercise and its effects influence how the individuals construct their social identities. The media effects examined continue to include parasocial relationships building within the Kuwaiti society, through a gender lens as well, and the influence this posits on the individuals and society as a whole. Media effects are also examined on a social front, with a closer look at notions of self-esteem and narcissism, and how social identities are reflected online.

As published in the Mediterranean Journal of Social Sciences –Volume 5, Issue 23, November 2014–Pages 1906-1913.

The Relationship Among TV Violence, Aggression, Anti-Social Behaviors and Parental Mediation

Juliet Dinkha, American University of Kuwait, Associate Professor of Psychology, jdinkha@auk.edu.kw & Charles Mitchell, Independent Researcher, Charlesamitchell@gmail.com PO box 3323 Safat Kuwait, 13034

Abstract

This paper proposes to ascertain whether there is a correlation between parent-child relationships and media consumption in Kuwait, and if so, it will examine the factors that play a role in it such as the parents' education level, marital status, and socioeconomic status (SES). In our research we attempt to find out whether when there is less parental supervision and interaction if this will lead children into consuming more television and whether more television consumption will lead adolescents to assume anti-social behaviors, most notably violent behaviors. We built on the theory of modeling and social learning and the effects on violence, seminally noted in the work by Albert Bandura, and theorized that we would also find correlations with TV consumption and violent behaviors in our sample. We wrote, assembled and circulated a qualitative survey based on the literature review consisting of personal interviews of 120 respondents and asked them about their childhood relationship with TV, violent behavior, and their parents' control of their TV consumption. We wrote our results as a narrative based on the responses in our sample. What we found in our results was that a large number of adolescents in Kuwait were exhibiting violent behaviors directly correlated to the amount of violent content they consumed on TV as a child especially when there was little parental control or mediation, this was especially true with the male respondents in our sample.

Keywords: violence, Kuwait, TV, modeling theory, social learning theory.

1. TV consumption, child development, and aggression

By the time children are 3-years old they are consuming on average of two to three hours of television per day. Children spend more time with the television remote control than they do behind their desks at schools. More than 1000 research studies have examined and drawn correlations between children's TV consumption and violent behaviors, but direct causation has never been established (Black 1995). It is generally believed that TV viewings affects children in four primary ways: 1. Leading to imitation of what they see 2. Reducing their sensitivity to violent themes and images, 3. Mitigating the effect of other external agents on the moral ramifications of violent behavior and 4. Creating or increasing arousal. However, many of these studies also posit that there are many other environmental variables and most likely a mix of these variables leads to aggressive behaviors. Children's ages, cognitive ability, and parenting are fundamental to the way each child interprets TV violence. The consensus of the wealth of investigations into the effects of TV violence on children posits that the more hours a child spends consuming TV messages the greater the correlation between TV viewing and aggressive attitudes and behaviors (Black 1995; Murray 2008).

Most of the research into this field has been accumulated in the Western world, with Britain, Canada, and the United States among the primary pioneers. This westernization of the effects of TV and violence leads to a deficit in the body of research in developing nations such as Kuwait. The accumulated data throughout this particular inquiry examines the following questions: Does the relationship between parent/guardian and child affect the child's level of media consumption and the behavior of the child? It is hypothesized that healthy and secure relationships between parent/guardian and child may indicate a stronger sense of attentiveness from parent/guardian and obedience from child, indicating less TV consumption and pro-social behavior in the child. Meanwhile, weak relationships between parent/guardian and child may indicate lack of attentiveness from parent/guardian and rebellion from child, indicating more TV consumption and anti-social behavior.

A number of possible factors that may play a role in the correlation between parent-child relationships and TV consumption including the parents' socio-economic status (SES), education, and social class. In addition, the parent's own television viewing habits and attitudes and knowledge regarding the child's viewing can also be another variable that plays a role in this correlation. A number of theories suggest that the parent's beliefs about the realism of television violence might aggravate or alleviate how television affects the child. Furthermore, whether the parent watches what the child watches might indicate the parent's concern and attitudes about television's effect on his or her children. Moreover, a number of experimental studies suggest that intervention by an adult might moderate the effect TV violence has on the child (Hicks 1968; Huesmann, Lagerspetz, Eron 1984). However, no evidence of such an effect has been reported in a field study. Similarly, it raises the question whether television-viewing habits can be passed on from parent to child. There is some evidence that it is possible (Soneson, 1979; von Feilitzen, 1976), but it does not answer the question regarding the possibility of parents who watch more violence also have children who watch more violence (Huesmann et al., 1984).

The article *Imitating Life, Imitating Television: The Effects of Family and Television Models on Children's Moral Reasoning* by Marina Krcmar and Edward T. Vieira, Jr. (2005) focuses more on how children's viewing habits and parent-child relationship may affect their acquisition of morality. One example of this is that children imitate certain behaviors either from family or television. According to Krcmar, Vieira, Jr (2005) one of the five keys of good parenting is modeling, since the parents are considered role models for their children's character development. When parents demonstrate positive behaviors in front of their children, the children themselves will be motivated to model the behavior.

However, it's not only parents that children are modeling. Modeling falls under the social learning theory paradigm. The theory asserts that parents, peers, role models, and the mass media acts as an agent of socialization, for which behaviors are imitated. One six months study, sponsored by American television network CBS sampled more than 1500 school age boys and investigated the relationship between their aggressive behaviors and their television viewing habits. Of the 12 percent (188 boys) who were involved in 10 or more acts of violence over that period, boys who consumed more TV violence had been engaged in the more serious acts of violence (Murray 2008). However, another 1982 study by the US broadcaster NBC published in Murray (2008) surmises no direct correlations between television consumption and violence in a large sample of boys. "On the basis of the analyses we carried out to test for such a causal connection there is no evidence that television exposure has a consistently significant effect on subsequent aggressive behavior in the [elementary school] sample of boys" pg 1218. Still, one the longest studies on the topic repudiates the NBC data and concurs with the 1978 CBS investigation. Researchers followed school children for 10 years from the ages of eight to 18. Children were questioned about their viewing habits, favorite shows. Peer ratings were collected to establish their aggressive behaviors and violent content in their favorite programs was also measured across the two time periods. What researchers found was that exposure to early television violence was a factor in producing violent behaviors in later years. Other studies found early onset of aggressive behaviors. Several investigations concluded that violence in cartoons led to increased violence in children's playrooms (Murray 2008).

A wide body of cross sectional surveys over the last 50 years have reached the conclusion that physical aggression is directly correlated to the amount of television a child consumes on TV and in film (Anderson 2003). These surveys have had different methodologies, examined children in across a diverse sample of ages and many have found children and adolescents who were consuming TV images engaging in violent behavior no matter their gender. Some of the research examined, however, noted that aggression was particularly prevalent in children but less so when examined in older children or young adults. The sheer volume of the data seen in a comprehensive meta-analysis of 410 research studies published between 1957 and 1990 find strong correlations between TV consumption of violent images and violent behaviors in children. However, some research still indicates that violent content does still affect older audiences such as teenagers and young adults

19 or older, which leads to conclusion that even in older children — teens and adults —the effect of TV violence is still tangible. Some studies has even found strong connections between news programming and violence, especially suicide rates, with reports on suicides often times leading to increased likelihood that some viewers may take their own lives (Anderson 2003).

While the breadth of preceding studies have directly addressed the issue of TV and violence in children and adolescents, as Black (1995) postulates, other socialization agents are factors in how a child interprets and expresses violence, including the relationship between parent and child. A paramount dynamic in the parent-child relationship and its connection with media violence is whether open communication is present in areas of mediating conflicting morals. Ideally, if there is open, honest, and respectful communication between parent and child, then the child will develop coping methods to control moral dilemmas and will additionally empathize with other perspectives on these issues. Accordingly, parent-child communication and control determines how a child would emulate certain behaviors from television, and increases crystallizing of morals (Krcmar et. al 2005).

Consequently, many argue that the parent-child relationship plays an imperative role in whether children model certain behaviors seen on television. Ingunn Hagen (2007) suggests methods for parents and their children to determine how much television a child should consume. Some of the methods used to regulate TV consumption include children seeking parental permission to watch television and specifying how long they can watch TV. The parents' role is to decide how much TV and what programs are appropriate for their children of different ages, or even relegating TV viewing for after their child has finished doing their homework. In essence, the parents' biggest concern mostly pertained to how children use their time. Interestingly, one of the respondents in the study said that asking his parents to video tape his favorite cartoon after his bedtime is how he bypasses this rule. In another case, an 11-year-old subject says that he goes to be at 9 pm and thus could not watch anything after that time. In other cases, parents would divert their children's attention by asking them to play outdoors or to take a break from being in the house. Along this line, another family reported that the reason behind their 'no TV before 6pm rule' is due to a desire to keep the children busy, since they believe that children should have interests outside of TV viewing for better development of critical thinking and motor skills (Hagen 2007).

Other researchers have also delved into the subject of parental intervention and supervision of TV consumption, specifically looking at the how to help children cope with messages from television advertisements. Some of these proposed methods included implementing more public regulation of advertisements, tuning into more TV programs targeted at children and encouraging parents to become more involved with their children's TV habits (Walsh, Laczniak, & Carlson, 2000). The authors suggest that parents become more involved by watching TV with their children in order to help them distinguish the differences between a TV program and an advertisement; however, the authors conclude that often times children consume TV without any parental supervision. Correspondingly, there are four types of parenting styles: Neglecting, Indulgent, Authoritarian, and Authoritative, suggesting that the type of parenting style used may have an effect on their children and their TV viewing habits. For instance, neglectful parents do not pay attention to what their children watch on TV since they are not actively involved with their children and are not very restrictive. Indulgent parents (also known as permissive) parents, try to remove as many external restraints to their children's behaviors, as possible, while at the same time ensuring their children's wellbeing. They are generally characterized as very involved with their children, and give them their rights and space, but not all the responsibilities that come with being more independent. Unlike indulgent parents, Authoritarian parents tend to be stricter when interacting with their children: expecting children to obey without question and negating two-way communication. Authoritative parents are described as more willing to engage with their children directly and are warm, yet restrictive because they expect their children to act responsibly and to adhere to family rules. However, once the children are older they are allowed more independence and self-expression. (Walsh, Laczniak, & Carlson, 2000).

1.1 Methodology

Questionnaire consisting of 22-items was assembled based on the literature review (Table. 1). The survey was disseminated to 120 random respondents around Kuwait via face-to-face interviews personal interviews. The respondents were asked to answer the survey based on their experiences with TV, violent behavior and their parents' mediation of their TV consumption until they were 16 years of age. We utilized student assistants to circulate and administer the survey. We surveyed subjects up to the age of 30 as we wanted clearer recollection of childhood memories with TV and violent behavior, so we found it practical to cap the age of our respondents. Although the survey was face to face, consisting of personal interviews the names of the respondents were not recorded but the standard demographic questions were asked. The survey was initially pre-tested on 30 randomly selected individuals who live in Kuwait. Comments about questions they found irrelevant or could not answer such as violent sports, violent video games played in Kuwait or if it was not culturally understood, items were deleted or modified. The pretesting questions allowed us to validate and modify the survey before finally distributing to our sample. We randomly looked for participants between 18 and 30 years of age who could recall the type of TV shows they watched and who could recall how their parents mediated TV viewing. As previously stated, this study aimed to address the correlation between children's TV/ media violence viewing habits and its relation to aggressive behaviors in Kuwait. This research also explored the effects of parental mediation of TV consumption on child, adolescent and adult violence.

Table .1

1. How did your parents monitor what you watched on TV when you were a child?
2. Explain any restrictions in how many hours of TV you watched as a child?
3. What were you allowed to and not allowed to watch on TV when you were a child?
4. What activities did your parents encourage you to participate in besides watching TV?

5. What activities did you do with your parents?
6. How many hours of your leisure time as a child did you spend participating in activities with your parents?
7. Were you attracted to violent cartoons when you were younger? Such as: Action shows, rough sports shows like wrestling, American football or martial arts or cartoons such as X men, the Road Runner and Tom and Jerry? (*If yes continue to 8, if no skip to 10*)
8. Why do you think you watched violent TV shows when you were younger ?
9. How many hours of your leisure time did you spend watching films and TV shows with violent themes when you were a child?
10. On the scale of 1-10, how many programs that you watched as child would you say contained fighting, guns or aggressive behavior such as shouting, this includes sports?
11. Do you currently watch TV shows with violent themes such as action shows or cartoons? (*if yes continue to 12 if no skip to 13*)
12. What percentage of the shows that you watch *now* do you consider to have violent themes?
13. When you were younger did your friends consider you to be tough and aggressive? (*if yes continue to 14 if none skip to 16*)
14. Why did you friends consider you to be tough and aggressive when you were a child (Please explain in detail and provide clear examples of behavior?)
15. Please describe aggressive behaviors you had as a child such as fights, shoving, bullying or arguments.
16. How many times over the last year have you gotten into an aggressive interactions such as road rage, fights or arguments? *(If none skip to question 19 if yes continue to 17)*
17. Can you describe these incidents and how and why they took place?
18. Did your parents ever tell you that TV was having a negative effect on your behavior Please explain what your parents said. (*if yes, continue if no skip to 20*)
19. How many hours of your leisure time did you spend playing violent video games such as GTA, WWE, when you were a child?

20. What kinds of aggressive or contact sports did you participate in as a child such as wrestling, kick boxing or American football? *(if none skip to 22 if yes continue to 21)*
21. Did your parents encourage you to participate in these sports or were these your choices? Please explain fully.
22. What effects do you think shows with violent themes and characters have had on your behavior over the years?

1.1.1 Findings &Narratives

After administering our survey to 120 subjects we are reporting the most significant findings. As part of our method, we wanted our participants to define violent behaviors themselves. Many respondents indicated that violent television had no effect on their behavior in numerous instances, and they failed to see that some behaviors were in fact violent acts. Case in point, some respondents, did not consider road rage as violent and perceived their aggressive behaviors and actions behind the wheel as justified, while others understood road rage as a clear act of aggression. One 18 year old subject said, "Over the years, I haven't gotten into aggressive interactions such as road rage, fights, or arguments," but at the same time he further asserted, "I think shows with violent themes and characters haven't had any effect on me since I didn't use to watch shows with violent themes." This demonstrates the lack of understanding with some respondents the correlation effect between violent content and violent behavior.

The respondents who reported parental mediation and control of their TV viewing had a greater understanding of violence but reported that often times it was only romantic and sexual themes that were censored by their parents. This mode of television mediation by parents is in line with Kuwait's censorship paradigm, where the Ministry of Information censors mainly romantic and sexual content on state own and run television channels. Inappropriate content is often deleted including kissing and intimate scenes. Conversely, violent shows are aired on TV uncensored in Kuwait and males are often allowed to watch these programs because they are associated with masculinity.

In our responses, clear contrasts were often seen with gender roles and aggression between males and females. Females seem to be more reserved and hesitant to share information that would label them as aggressive and males were more open to admitting their aggressiveness. Many females did not report having consumed any violent content as children and many said aggressive behaviors were acts they observed more in males and felt that violence on TV affected males more than it did themselves or other females: "Shows with violent themes have not affected my behavior, but it has impacted many other children especially the male gender," said a 30-year old female respondent.

Parents generally controlled what females watched on TV, while males were given more autonomy in this respect: "I was restricted from watching horror images or videos that could disturb my mentality or adult movies or videos. My parents would usually change the channel or fast forward it," one 21-year old female reported.

It was observed that parents of male respondents; however, were more likely to have given consent whether explicitly or tacitly for their male children to consume media violence since it is seen as masculine. Males often played with toys that encouraged violence such as fake guns and swords. However, female respondents received negative reaction from parents if they viewed violent cartoons or engaged in aggressive playing. Females generally described being directed toward what was seen as more gender appropriate activities such as playing with dolls or watching programs that were more considered more suitable for young girls such as Disney cartoons, which lacked the violence of action shows and superhero cartoons that are often aimed at a male audience.

Many females were also directed toward participating in outside home activities more aligned with traditional gender roles: "I was pushed into swimming which I really loved... Also, drawing was something they perceived as a feminine activity that I could safely and easily waste my time doing," said a 21-year old female who reported her parents encouraged her to engage in activities aside from viewing TV that were imbued with stereotypical female attributes. Females recounting violent behavior were very low in our study but one female in our sample reported regular acts of violent behavior. She described herself as being the bully in the family who routinely beat up her younger brother and cousins. The 24-year old also correlates her TV viewing with her aggressive nature: "I think watching a lot of WWF (World Wrestling Federation), made me think I can fight and made me think as a child that I was able to fight like them, which made me excited and always wanting to wrestle with my friends and cousins."

While females are often discouraged from engaging in such aggressive behaviors and restricted from watching aggressive content, many times males reported that they were often encouraged to participate in physical and aggressive sports such as kick boxing, karate and soccer. Furthermore, the males in our sample were generally allowed to consume more violent TV programming than females. An 18 year old male respondent, for example, rated the amount of shows he watched that contained violent themes on a scale of 0-10. He described most of the shows he watched as an 8 for violent content. Another participant recalled playing out several violent scenes that he saw on TV without getting in trouble at home. However, when asked does he believe viewing media violence effects his behavior now as an adult, his answer was no. "I was a child then and now am an adult."

Nevertheless, some males did report that their parents took an interest in the content they were viewing on television and had strict rules and policies in place about what they could and couldn't watch. "My parents monitored me by sitting with me while I watched and showed me beneficial channels. They were aware of me and aware of what I am watching. For example, they even taught me how to pick up the main point from the beneficial channels and how to use the TV in a positive way because once I learned how to use it from the childhood, automatically I will know how to use it at this current age," said one 21-year old male respondent. Correspondingly, this subject further reported that he does not recollect exhibiting any aggressive tendencies as a child and his friends never considered him to be tough and aggressive.

His story reflects our findings that there is a strong correlation between parental supervision and child aggression with less violence reported in households where parents actively engaged in mediation. The parental control methods reported were locking the channels, expressing verbally what sort of shows were inappropriate to watch, co-viewing and encouraging children to pursue other activities. "As a child, I think these shows had a small influence on my behavior. I used to be short tempered, and I believe that my interest in these shows and games had an effect on that. However, as I grew up, these influences faded away, though I still enjoy watching violent themed movies," said a 21-year old male. His parents generally discouraged violent TV viewing and even though he was a male and did watch some violent TV he said he tended to grow out of any aggressive influences TV seemed to have on him.

Several of the participants mentioned that their parents did not set guidelines or supervise what they consumed. Respondents who reported little or no parental supervision, also reported more exposure to violent content and exhibited such behaviors in many instances: "My friends used to consider me to be tough and aggressive because I was short tempered and could not take any offense; therefore would usually get into arguments and sometimes fights…I remember getting into a lot of arguments and rarely into fist fights," said a 24-year old male respondent who reported that his parents did not monitor what he watched on television when he was younger. Similar patterns in behavior were reported in a 21-year old who consumed three hours of TV per day, many of which he said contained violent content: "My friends considered me aggressive and tough because I had aggressive tendencies. I was physically aggressive and I did things like punching. I also ordered people around…As a child, my aggressive behavior was physical like shoving, punching, and kicking." One 27-year old male, "Ali" (not his real name) recalled that his parents had strict rules on what he could consume when he was younger; however, he ranked the amount of shows that he watched that contained violence as 10 of out 10. He also admits he consumed violent content on TV specifically because he wanted to be strong and to model the violent behaviors he observed. He said that he would imitate these characters and they made him want to fight.

Like Ali, 30-year old Ahmed (not his real name) also reported severe incidents of violence: "I was considered to be one of the toughest as a kid. I was a trouble maker and I would always end up in fights. I realize now because I was a tiny boy, I needed to prove myself within my peer circles. I would never miss out on a fight, and I would always stand up for my friends. As an example, when I was about 20, my little cousin, at the age of 14, would always be bullied by the neighborhood kids because he had a smooth beautiful face and kids saw him as soft rather than a man. And one time he came home and his clothes were dirtied and he was a mess he had a frustrated face. He told me that some older guys were harassing him and I got angry. I went over to their house, found them around the neighborhood and straight on advanced aggressively I pounded the first guy and kept pounding on him, me on top and him under me. The others reacted in trying to get me off, but I just continued what I was doing not seeing anything else. When a lot of people started to gather, I lifted him, pushed him through the crowd and into his house and that's when people starting fighting me back and I went home drenched in blood. There were many other incidents where I went home in blood and was driven to the emergency room more than I can count because of my aggressive behavior."

Despite these incidents, Ahmed however, said he didn't consider TV to have had an impact on his violent tendencies but still he recounted heavy TV viewing as child and that he was attracted to shows that contained violent themes and this continued into his adolescence: "Yes, what I watched majorly was violent shows, considering I am a male, and they included sport shows like wrestling and boxing, also many cartoon shows that depicted violence. As I grew, I started watching more and more TV shows that promoted violence too, like shows about soldiers or shows that showed the criminals of history."

Another male respondent, whose parents did monitor what he watched on TV, felt that TV still had an effect on him but in a positive light: "I believe these shows (violent shows) have educated me on the consequences associated with violent behavior. I also believe that I personally benefitted from these shows because they represented part of a wide spectrum of television shows with varying themes in which I was giving insight into the mechanics of the world," the 18-year old said.

In contrast to Ali and Ahmed, a few male respondents reported very little parental supervision but also noted they did not feel the pressure to watch violent shows and did not necessarily gravitate toward violent content on TV. However, these males, like Ali and Ahmed, found that the violent content they consumed did have an impact on how they exhibited violence in their adolescent stage: "I didn't used to watch violent things when I was a kid but still when I grew up I found it necessary to defend myself and my family and my friends and I started to act aggressively when needed. So I used violent aggressive shows as a way to solve problems later," reported an 18-year old male.

In some cases the respondents in our sample described that they felt TV had contributed to negative behaviors but not necessarily violent ones and some note that their parents had pointed out these detrimental habits, and this was especially true with our female respondents: "Yes, my parents told me that TV was having a negative effect on my behavior because it was distracting me from my studies and was making me lazy," a female reported. Another female, 25, also reported negative behaviors that were not necessarily violent but felt were the result of the modeling behaviors from TV: "Violence was never a focus in the TV shows I would watch. However, in general when I saw a way a character handled a situation, it might have encouraged me to act the same way, and I would even go as much as saying that I thought it was acceptable. For example, if a kid was cheating and decided to write answers on his shoes, I might have been encouraged to try such method and see where it takes me."

While the vast majority of our respondents, even the ones with high levels of violent TV consumption and violent behavior, did not blame this on the influence of TV, there were a few participants who highlighted TV as the primary agent that influenced their violent behaviors. But almost all the these respondents also said that while TV made them more violent, that was not necessarily bad, as they are more able to defend themselves, and in many cases their families. This was especially reported among the male respondents, with one 22-year old male explaining, "It (TV) affected me both negatively and positively. Negatively because I 've become a somewhat aggressive person and positively because now I'm strong enough to look out for myself and be brave." Yet another 22- year old male subject reported being unashamed or even proud of his violent demeanor, he described regular acts of violence at school when he was younger, which included being the class bully along with his friends. The group of boys would pick on other kids and beat on each other and often times he ended up being suspended from school. He readily admits that TV was a major influence on his behavior but he doesn't regret that influence and asserts that TV "has made me the man I am today."

1.1.1.1 Conclusion

In our study we noticed several trends across our interviews: There were stark differences between males and females and how they assimilated and modeled violent behaviors seen on television. Males were often allowed to consume violent content because this is recognized as more masculine while females were often discouraged from violent content as culturally these are seen as a inappropriate for young girls. Males who watched large amounts of TV often engaged in violent acts but did not interpret this behavior as being influenced by TV viewing. It is assumed that this denial could be cultural socialization where it's better to be influenced by parents and friends than by an external influence that is not inherent in the society. Men in Kuwait are socialized to be strong and admitting to the influence of television may be perceived as a sign of weakness since TV is dominated by western programming and not traditional Arab or Kuwaiti values. However, the males that did admit to the violent influence of TV utilized the collectivist culture to justify their aggression saying they needed to defend their families, which is a fundamental role for males in Kuwait. Moreover, we noticed females more likely to model deviant behaviors such as cheating or neglecting their studies and being lazy. These are traits often are acceptable for females in this society to exhibit. When parental mediation was present, respondents reported less violent modeling as they were able to reconcile fact from fiction and understand the consequences of aggressive behaviors.

References

Anderson, C. A., Berkowitz, L., Donnerstein, E., Huesmann, L. R., Johnson, J. D., Linz, D., & Wartella, E. (2003). The influence of media violence on youth. *Psychological science in the public interest*, 4(3), 81-110.

Bandura, A., Ross, D., & Ross, S. A. (1961). Transmission of aggression through imitation of aggressive models. *The Journal of Abnormal and Social Psychology*, 63(3), 575.

Bandura, A., & Walters, R. H. (1963). Social learning and personality development.

BBC.com. (May 2013) *Kuwait Profile*. Retrieved June 15 from http://www.bbc.com/news/world-middle-east-14646837

Black, D., Newman, M., (1995) Television Violence and Children: Its Effects Need To Be Seen In The Context of Other Influences on Children's Mental Health. *BMJ: British Medical Journal*, Vol. 310, No. 6975), pp. 273-274

Davies, J. J., & Gentile, D. A. (2012). Responses to children's media use in families with and without siblings: A family development perspective. *Family Relations*, 61(3), 410-425.

Dominick, Joseph, R (2009). The Dynamics of Mass Communication: Media in the Digital Age. New York, NY: *McGraw-Hill*

Eron, L. E. (1982). Parent-child interaction, television violence, and aggression of children. *American Psychologist*, 37(2), 197-211.

Gentile, D. A., Nathanson, A. I., Rasmussen, E. E., Reimer, R. A., & Walsh, D. A. (2012). Do you see what I see? Parent and child reports of parental monitoring of media. *Family Relations*, 61, 470-487.

Hagen, I. (2007). We can't just sit the whole day watching TV': Negotiations concerning media use among youngsters and their parents. *Young, 15*(4), 369-393.

Hajeeh, M., & Lairi, S. (2009). Marriage partner selection in Kuwait: An analytical hierarchy process approach. *Journal of Mathematical Sociology, 33*(3), 222-240.

Hicks, D. J. (1968). Effects of co-observer's sanctions and adult presence on imitative aggression. Child Development, 39(1), 303-309.

Hopf, W. H., Huber, G. L., & Weiß, R. H. (2008). Media violence and youth violence: A 2-year longitudinal study. *Journal of Media Psychology: Theories, Methods, and Applications,* 20(3), 79- 96.

Huesmann, R. L., Lagerspetz, K., & Eron, L. D. (1984). Intervening variables in the TV violence-aggression relation: Evidence from two countries . *Developmental Psychology, 20*(5), 746-775.

Kirmayer, L., Lemelson, R., & Barad, M. (2007) Understanding Trauma: Integrating Biological, Clinical, and Cultural Perspectives. New York: Cambridge University Press.

Krcmar, M., & Vieira, Jr., E. T. (2005). Imitating life, imitating television: The effects of family and television models on children's moral reasoning. *Communication Research, 32*(3), 267-294.

Martins, N., & Harrison, K. (2012). Racial and gender differences in the relationship between children's television use and self-esteem: a longitudinal panel study. *Communication Research, 39*(3), 338-357.

Mitchell, C., Dinkha, A., Kononova, A., Rashwan, T., Matta, M., (2014). A Body of Dissatisfaction: A Study of the Effects of Media Imperialism in Kuwait, *American Journal of Humanities and Social Sciences,* Vo1. 2, No. 1, 2014, 76-87

Murray, J. P. (2008). Media violence the effects are both real and strong. American Behavioral Scientist, 51(8), 1212-1230.

Myers, D. (2012). Social Relations. *Social Psychology* (ED 10). McGraw Hill.

Reporters Without Borders, *World Press Freedom Index - 2013*, (2013) retrieved from: http://www.refworld.org/docid/5108f621e.html, retrieved, 28 June 2014

Shah, N. M., Badr, H. E., Yount, K., & Shah, M. A. (2011). Decline in co-residence of parents and children among older Kuwaiti men and women: What are the significant correlates?. *Cross Cultural Geronotology*, 26(2), 157-174.

Von Feilitizen,C (1976). The functions served by the mass media. In R .Brown (Ed.), *Children and television* (pp. 90-115) London. Collier-Macmillan.

Walsh, A. D., Laczniak, R. N., & Carlson, L. (1998). Mothers' preferences for regulating children's television. *27*(3), 23-36.

Werner, Sonia Soneson,. Affect and Moral Judgment in Older Children. Thesis. N.d. N.p.: n.p., 1979. Print.

Wheeler, D. (2000). New media, globalization, and Kuwaiti national identity. *Middle East Journal*, 54(3), 432-444.

As published in the American Journal of Humanities and Social Sciences – Volume 2, Issue 1, January 2014– Pages 76-87.

A Body of Dissatisfaction: A Study of the Effects of Media Imperialism on Body Image in Kuwait

Charles Mitchell, American University of Kuwait,
charlesamitchell@gmail.com
Juliet Dinkha, American University of Kuwait
jdinkha@auk.edu.kw
Anastasia Kononova, American University of Kuwait
kononovaa@gmail.com
Tasneem Rashwan, American University of Kuwait
tasneem.rashwan@hotmail.com
Monica Matta, American University of Kuwait
mmatta@auk.edu.kw

Abstract

Media has an enduring reputation of affecting perception. Perpetuating unrealistic body standards is just one-way mediated messages influence negatively an audience. In the last 25 years, Kuwait has seen an invasion of western media including TV, music, magazines and movies. We decided to tackle the subject of the effects of this cultural imperialism to see if the prevalence of these imported western body images were having a negative impact. The social comparison theory states that individuals evaluate themselves through comparison even with media images. This study examines how Western — mainly — U.S. media imperialism and the social comparison theory through media affects body perception by examining the effects of college-age young adults watching shows with prominent thin television characters compared to shows that had prominent average body types in the cast. We expect to find that exposure to programming with only thin characters will correlate with body dissatisfaction. The study included distributing 286 self-administered preliminary surveys to discover the most popular shows that college students (mostly 18 to 25 year olds) watched. After we identified the most popular shows, blind self-administered surveys were circulated to a sample of 240 college-age young adults (120 males and 120 females) to determine if any correlation could be made between their television show preferences and their body dissatisfaction. We found body image dissatisfaction is being reported, leading to the implication that media imperialism is eroding traditional Arab body image in Kuwait.

Keywords: body image, media imperialism, cultural imperialism, social comparison theory, Kuwait

Cultural and Media Imperialism

Media imperialism is a mode of thought that asserts that foreign culture invades countries through the dissemination of mediated messages such as television, radio, magazines, movies, Internet and music (Dominick 2009). Kuwait struggles between two worlds: it has a strong nationalistic identity with coexists with an overabundance of foreign new media technology (Wheeler 2000).

The American mass media is widely exported to other nations such as Kuwait and the concern is that these countries, many being developing, will have their own cultural values and traditions eroded and replaced with American mores and viewpoints. This phenomenon leaves room for inquiry and research on the impact these messages are having politically, for example, the influence on democratic movements or socially, including impact on music, fashion, art, language, and lastly body image, which is the focus of our inquiry.

Critics say that American values and the American point of view is becoming dominant across much of the world due to the exportation of Hollywood films, TV shows and international news based out of the United States. Not only in Kuwait but there are numerous examples: case in point, US exported news coverage about regions such as South America, that are often portrayed as in involved with drug trafficking and revolutions, as these are issues that primarily affect US interests and US audiences. In many countries US media has displaced or/and eroded the local media, that are unable to compete with the demand and marketing dollars of US entertainment. To this extent, many countries that see the danger of cultural/media imperialism have placed media quotas on US entertainment content to help offset the damage done to their own domestic media industries and to hinder possible cultural influence and degradation (Dominick 2009).

Petras (1994) asserts that cultural imperialism has two main goals: to gain an economic foothold on foreign markets and the other being political and to shape audiences through cultural hegemony. Cultural imperialism consciously works to separate the audience from their own cultural heritage and traditions. In his article, Petras makes the point that audiences are largely working class who see US media as a way of assimilating a desirable modern lifestyle. The author postulates that the message is often directed toward young people who are more susceptible to the influences of mediated messages. The youth are the primary market of US media imperialism not only because they are the most lucrative demographic, but because they are the most attracted to US consumerism and ideas of individualism (Petras 1994):

> Petras discovered the following: In relation to the third world, cultural imperialism can be defined as the systematic penetration and domination of the cultural life of the popular classes by the ruling class of the west in order to reorder the values, behavior, institutions and identity of the oppressed peoples to conform with the interests of the imperial classes (p. 2070)

However, there isn't a popular consensus on the definition of media imperialism (Fejes 1981). In his article Fejes, articulates that media imperialism emerged from the dependency model as opposed to modernization theories. Modernization revolves around the development of social values, while the dependency model focuses on the relationship between developed and underdeveloped nations, and the problems that arise from that link: underdeveloped nations are at a disadvantage in a political and economic system that favors developed nations. Modernization theorists view the developing countries as evolving social ideas and ideals on a continuum with western industrial nations as the archetype of where this evolution will eventually culminate.

No matter the definition, the influence of media imperialism especially on body image is prevalent and empirical. A wide body of studies have deduced strong causal relationships to substantiate its influence. One three-year study of body image of Fijian women, after the introduction of television, discovered that western programming with the depictions of thin American ideals of beauty led to a precipitous increase in bulimic behavior among teenage girls in the country. Moreover, the Fijian females' sense of being beautiful had also decayed dramatically due to US TV programming (Wykes & Gunter 2005). This has been the trend in other countries: In Italy where men often report to prefer full figured women, the influence of media imperialism on body image is again observable. Florentine women are now facing problems with perceptions of their bodies because of the prevalence of US media messages. This trend is especially pervasive among teenage girls. Furthermore, the rise of eyelid surgery, to mimic western features, is becoming increasingly commonplace amongst Asian women in far-east countries (Fedorak 2008).

Body Image

Body image dissatisfaction is the theory that individuals are unhappy with how they look in relation to their body. Researchers have been holding the media responsible for the rise in body image dissatisfaction in accordance with the sociocultural theory, which posits that people learn from social interaction. In the article, *Striving for Bodily Perfection? An Exploration of the Drive for Muscularity in Canadian Men (2003)* the authors of the study postulated that exposure to idealized male bodies would positively correlate with a desire to be more muscular and that men who use common social comparisons when evaluating their physical appearance will show a positive correlation with a desire to be more muscular. The researchers surveyed 310 male undergraduates enrolled in a community college and used the DMAQ scale (an 8-item scale that measures the desire to attain a more muscular body) and a modified USC scale to measure how much they use social comparisons (Hopkins, Morrison, Morrison 2003). The findings concluded that there was a strong correlation with fitness magazines showcasing ideal male body types and comparisons to universal standards of the idealized male form, with the strength of dedication of the respondents to attain muscularity.

Moreover, when one speculates how the media emphasizes unrealistic and aesthetic ideals, an image of a tall thin woman with perfectly groomed hair with unblemished skin often comes to mind, but studies have revealed that there has been an increase in emphasis on male aesthetic ideals in the media. In their paper, Jamie Farquhar and Louise Wasylkiw (2007) argue that since the 1980's the image of the male body has evolved to one that has been about the male form as a process, to where a man's physical appearance has now become an object. Now the focus is not on what the body can do but what the male body looks like. To test their hypothesis the authors performed a content analysis of a sample of male bodies in the ads lining the magazine Sports Illustrated, from 1975 to 2005 (Farquhar, Wasylkiw, 2007). The authors construed that since the 1970's there has been a steady and strong increase in the trend of conceptualization of men's body as an object, with a consistent surge in discrete male body parts across the sample of magazines.

In the past, the majority of research on body image dissatisfaction has focused on females who have consistently shown dissatisfaction with their bodyweight (Harrison 1997). However, research has been increasingly focusing on males' body dissatisfaction (Morry, Staska 2001; Agliata, Tantleff-Dunn, 2004; Hobza, Walker, Yakushko, Peugh 2007). Though studies have discovered that both males and females do experience discontent with their body image, they have also given light to the differences in how males and females evaluate their physical appearance. Furthermore, the studies also show that the predictors and effects of body dissatisfaction differ for males and females. One result of body dissatisfaction is eating disorders. Eating disorders have been established to be affected by exposure to various mediated messages resulting in body dissatisfaction. Kristen Harrison (2000), distributed a questionnaire to 366 adolescents in three age groups, 6th, 9th and 12th grades that measured their media exposure and their interest in the messages that promoted body improvement. To measure their eating-disorder symptomatology, specifically their risk of developing anorexia nervosa, Harrison used the Children's Eating Attitudes Test. Certain subscales from the Eating Disorders Inventory to measure bulimic symptomatology, body dissatisfaction and drive for thinness were utilized. Harrison hypothesized that exposure to thin-ideals through magazines and fat characters through television would produce body dissatisfaction among females and that exposure to media with fat characters would also negatively affect the male audience. She expected that males would be less affected by the male thin-ideal than the females. In her study, Harrison determined that exposure to fat-characters predicted the eating-disorder bulimia and anorexia for females. Surprisingly, exposure to fat-character themed shows also predicted body dissatisfaction and anorexia in young men. The findings of the effects of watching television shows were intriguing to Harrison and are further explored by our current study. The media has shown to be a reinforcing agent for individuals on the ideal body type, as well as a way for individuals to evaluate themselves. When audiences are exposed to thin ideal body images or fat-characters, they are at higher risk of becoming dissatisfied with their bodies (Harrison 2000; Hobza, Walker, Yakushko, Peugh 2007).

There are mountains of evidence that support the idea that exposure to mediated aesthetic ideals have an effect on behavior and attitudes. Anschutz, Van Strien and Engels (2011) discerned in their study of 124 female students that female students who practiced dietary restraint in their daily lives ate less snack food while watching a movie that had commercials with slim models and diet products. The researchers theorized that those who were concerned with or were watching their weight would eat less after consuming ads with thin actors and diet oriented products. And to control for the mood of the movie, the researchers measured the students' mood towards the movie itself. The authors concluded that restrained eaters were reminded of their eating behaviors when they were watching media content with commercials of slim models and diet products. As part of their study,

Farquhar et. al.(2007) also uncovered that viewing media that emphasizes and idealizes aesthetic attributes contributes to negative self-evaluations.

Furthermore, Grabe and Ward (2008) conducted a meta-analysis on research studies in 2008. Their data revealed that exposure to media that depicts the thin-ideal body is associated with body image dissatisfaction, internalization of the thin body ideal, eating behaviors and to a general sense of body image dissatisfaction in women. Grabe and Ward analyzed published papers such as experimental studies reporting media having a stronger effect on internalization of the thin ideal and eating disorder symptomatology than body dissatisfaction, while other studies show equal effects. Though the studies' results seem to vary, according to Grabe and Ward media exposure to a thin-ideal body is related to body image dissatisfaction in women.

Gender Differences

How the media influences men and women differently has emerged through numerous studies. One example is an investigation by Marian Morry and Sandra Staska (2001). The study's findings surmise that when women read beauty magazines they are more likely to internalize the body image of the models in the magazine, and these women's degree of internalization is also a predictor of self-objectification – the concept of viewing one's self as an object first and as a subject secondly. Consequently, individuals who self-objectify see themselves as entities that others judge by appearance, leading to a preoccupation with looks. For the female subjects in the Morry et al. study, internalization was also the only predictor of body dissatisfaction. Conversely, men would read fitness magazines and their degree of internalization of these ideal body type positively predicted body dissatisfaction. The researchers expected to find evidence for five hypotheses: 1) Men reading fitness magazines would internalize societal ideals and women reading fashion magazines would also internalize societal ideals. 2) Consuming magazines should link with self-objectification in both sexes and that internalization would regulate the self-objectification. 3) Consuming magazines would relate to body dissatisfaction, again regulated by internalization of societal archetypes. 4) An occurrence of eating issues should be observed, and mediated by internalization of societal archetypes. 5) Finally, reading fashion magazines (female respondents) and fitness magazines (male respondents) should produce a relationship with body shape dissatisfaction (Morry and Staska 2001). The researchers recruited 150 students and allocated a questionnaire that included five different scales: the Magazine Exposure Scale, Eating Attitudes Test, Self-Objectification Questionnaire, Socio-cultural Attitudes Towards Appearance Questionnaire, and Body Shape Questionnaire. The authors found that reading magazines was associated with internalizing societal ideals. For women reading magazines also predicted self-objectification. For men reading fitness magazines with a tendency towards internalizing, predicted body shape dissatisfaction but not eating problems, but when men read fitness magazines while being already dissatisfied with their body type, eating problems were present (Morry, Staska 2001; Stice, Schupak, Shaw, Stein 1994).

Other studies further show that when men are exposed to media images depicting muscular-ideal characters these messages definitively lowered their muscle satisfaction (Hopkins, Morrison, Morrison 2003). The authors surveyed 104 male students and showed them either 15 commercials that depicted men having muscular physiques with their shirts off or 15 commercials depicting men not particularly muscular and wearing clothing that hid their body type. Expecting to find that exposure to ideal-muscular body images on television would lead to an increase in body dissatisfaction, the researchers did indeed find that the men's dissatisfaction with their muscle size and physical attractiveness had increased while watching the muscular ideal commercials more than the control group (Hargreaves, Tiggermann 2009). Interestingly, though men's body-esteem is affected by exposure to muscular body types, their self-esteem was not affected (Hobza, Walker, Yakushko, Peugh 2007). However, certain studies says that when men are exposed to ideal image advertisements they become depressed, indicating that more research in the area is needed to reach a consensus on the subject (Agliata, Tantleff-Dunn, 2004). Case in point, when males are exposed to media ideals that emphasize performance attributes, it can contribute to self-evaluation (Farquhar & Wasylkiw, 2007).

A method to better understand how media exposure affects individuals is to study ways that can protect them from the harmful effects of thin body ideal exposure, such as eating disorders. For example, when women are exposed to average sized women in mediated messages this leads to less restrictive dieting habits (Fister & Smith 2004).

Internalization has been found to be an important factor in mediating body dissatisfaction in individuals (Morry, Staska 2001). Culture is indicated also to take a back seat to internalization, according to a study done on Asian-American women that deduced that those who internalized media messages on ideal body types reported lower self-esteem (Lau, Lum, Chronister, Forrest 2006).

Social Comparison Theory

The social comparison theory posits that individuals compare themselves to others in order to evaluate or to enhance some aspects of the self. The media is a primary agent of the social comparison theory. Researchers who examined this theory postulate that when individuals compares themselves on with universal standards of body image then negative effects on their own body image was often found (Morrison et al. 2003). Serving as a self-evaluation tool, the social comparison theory depends on whether the individual internalizes or differentiates his or herself compared to others who are viewed as superior or inferior (Suls, Martin& Wheeler 2002). A study conducted by Frisby (2004) examined how much race played a role, if any, in body image self-evaluation. She exposed African-American women who had different levels of body esteem to advertisements of thin, physically attractive, white and black models and gauged their self-esteem afterwards. She surmised that viewing Caucasian ideals did not lower the African-American women's self-evaluation regardless of the previous level of body image. However, when exposed to idealized black models, the black women who previously reported low body esteem now reported body dissatisfaction. Frisby's study argues that when black women are exposed to idealized images of women who are similar in racial makeup to themselves problems of self-esteem may surface

(Frisby 2004). In at look at male participants, Thornton and Moore (1993) investigated men's self-ratings of their physical attractiveness. The respondents were divided into groups and exposed either to the highly attractive models or less attractive models. As anticipated, the men who had been exposed to the highly attractive models reported high-levels of body dissatisfaction (Morrison et al. 2003).

The present study is investigating the media's influence on male and female body image dissatisfaction in an Arab country with a high prevalence of US media. The following are the hypotheses that we will prove in our research:

Hypotheses

1. The more respondents watch US TV shows, will lead to greater Appearance Evaluation
2. Comparable effects of TV shows on body dissatisfaction found in Western studies will be observed in our study in Kuwait.
3. Watching TV shows with skinny characters will lead to greater body dissatisfaction.
4. Female respondents will report greater body dissatisfaction than male respondents.
5. Respondents viewing shows with average body types will report less body dissatisfaction than those watching shows with skinny characters.

METHOD

Pretesting and Validation

First, 286 preliminary surveys was distributed to discover what were the most popular shows being watched by both male and female college students (mostly 18 to 25 year olds). We additionally validated our study by distributing a list of these TV shows to four-college age students (two females and two males) to see if dominant characters fell correctly into skinny and average body types for both Arabic and English-language TV shows. We used a

1 to 7 scale where 1 meant "not at all" matching the categorized body type and 7 meaning fitting the body type category "a lot". Because we utilized the Multidimensional Body-Self Relations Questionnaire appearance scale (MBSRQ-AS) by Cash, et al. (1985, 1986) and the widely used Sociocultural Attitudes Toward Appearance Scale (SATAQ-3) Heinberg, et al. (1995), we did not see any justification or need for additional pre-testing.

Sample

A blind (non-face to face) self-administered paper-and-pencil cross-sectional survey (N = 233) was circulated in several classes of a liberal arts college in Kuwait. More than three-quarters of the student sample (75.9%) reported they were Kuwaiti citizens, while the rest reported being nationals of other countries (one respondent did not report his/her nationality). About a half of the sample (48.9%) reported they were males. Seven respondents did not report their gender. Over the half of the respondents (50.4%) were from 21 to 24 years old; 46.1% reported they were 18-20 years of age, and 3.4% didn't report their age.

Procedure

A blind self-administered paper-and-pencil questionnaires were distributed in a number of classes to ensure higher response rate. The survey was administered in English, which is the official language of the university where the study was administered.

MEASURES

TV show viewing

Before identifying how often respondents viewed certain television shows, we first generated the list of shows, both Western and Arabic, which were the most popular among the college students. For this purpose, 286 students were surveyed. Based on the students' responses, the list of 21 most viewed TV showed was created. Nine of these shows were Western (predominantly American, such as "How I Met Your Mother", "Modern Family", "The Office",

MEDIA EVOLUTION

among others), and 11 were produced in the Middle East (e.g., Noor (نور), Ajial (أجيال), Al-Ghareeb (الغريب)). Each respondent rated on a scale from 0 ("Never") to 3 ("Often") how often he/she viewed each of the selected shows.

Viewing Western and Arabic shows. The responses to the questions about show viewing were averaged separately for Western shows and Arabic shows. As a result, two continuous variables, *Viewing Western Shows* and *Viewing Arabic Shows*, were computed.

Viewing shows with skinny characters. Four coders rated each show on a scale from 1 ("not at all") to 7 ("a lot") with regards to how skinny its characters were. Shows with the highest rating were considered as *shows depicting skinny characters*. Viewing scores for these shows were averaged to create a single variable. To account for possible gender difference in perceptions of characters' skinniness, two male coders and two female coders rated the shows separately (intercoder reliability for males: Pearson correlation = .75, $p<.001$, intraclass correlation = .74, $p<.001$, Chronbach α = .85; intercoder reliability for females: Pearson correlation = .69, $p<.001$, intraclass correlation = .68, $p<.001$; Chronbach α = .81).

Viewing shows with average-body characters. Four coders rated each show on a scale from 1 ("not at all") to 7 ("a lot") with regards to average body types its characters had. Shows with the highest rating were considered as *shows depicting average-body characters*. The overall variable was computed based on the viewing scores for these shows. As in the previous case, gender differences in perceptions of characters' body averageness were taken into consideration. Two male coders and two female coders rated the shows separately (intercoder reliability for males: Pearson correlation = .79, $p<.001$, intraclass correlation = .79, $p<.001$, Chronbach α = .88; intercoder reliability for females: Pearson correlation = .74, $p<.001$, intraclass correlation = .74, $p<.001$, Chronbach α = .85).

Due to the fact that each show was rated on two scales representing characters' skinniness or body averageness, some shows were rated high on both.

Such shows were excluded from the analysis.

We also used The Multidimensional Body-Self Relations Questionnaire appearance scale (MBSRQ-AS) by Cash, et al. (1985, 1986) a 34-item self-report appearance focused inventory for the assessment of self-evaluation and orientation of five subsets that excludes fitness and health items, which are found in the larger, more comprehensive questionnaire. The shorter questionnaire measures Appearance Orientation, Appearance Evaluation, Overweight Preoccupation, Self-Classified Weight, and body area satisfaction.

Appearance Orientation. Appearance Orientation that represented extent of investment in one's appearance was measured with the use of 12 items (Cronbach's alpha = .74 for males; .72 for females, Cash et al., 1985, 1986). The respondents rated each of the 12 statements on a scale from 1 ("strongly disagree") to 7 ("strongly agree"). Then, one variable was computed by averaging scores for each of the 12 items.

Appearance Evaluation. Appearance Orientation conceptualized as the feeling of physical attractiveness or unattractiveness; satisfaction or dissatisfaction with one's looks was measured with the use of seven 7-point items (Cronbach's alpha = .61 for males; .79 for females, Cash et al., 1985, 1986). For each item, 1 corresponded to "strongly disagree" and 7 corresponded to "strongly agree." A single variable was calculated by averaging scores for each of the seven items.

Overweight Preoccupation. Overweight Preoccupation was defined as fat anxiety, weight vigilance, dieting, and eating restraint. This variable was calculated as an average of scores obtained with the use of four 7-point scales, where 1= "strongly disagree" and 7="strongly agree" (Cronbach's alpha =.66 for males; .75 for females, Cash et al., 1985, 1986).

Self-Classified Weight. Self-Classified Weight represented how one perceives and labels one's weight, from very underweight to very overweight. Two 7-point scales from 1 ("strongly disagree") to 7 ("strongly agree") were utilized to measure this variable (Cronbach's alpha =.66 for males; .78 for females, Cash et al., 1985, 1986).

Body Areas Satisfaction. Body Areas Satisfaction conceptualized as satisfaction with discrete aspects of one's appearance was measured with the use of nine items (Cronbach's alpha = .77 for males; .82 for females, Cash et al., 1985, 1986). The respondents rated each of the nine statements on a scale from 1 ("strongly disagree") to 7 ("strongly agree").

Lastly, we also distributed the Sociocultural Attitudes Toward Appearance Scale (SATAQ-3), which directly measures awareness and acceptance of cultural ideals of attractiveness. With this scale, we directly aim to gauge the impact of media messages on the level of General-Internalization; internalization from watching athletes, Pressures felt from aesthetic ideals, and if respondents look to general mediated messages such as film, TV and magazines for information about the ideal standards of appearance (Information). The following are descriptions of the variables used in this scale.

Internalization-General. Internalization-General meaning general influence of the media on perceived body size ideals was measured with the use of nine 5-point scales from 1 ("strongly disagree") to 5 ("strongly agree," Cronbach's alpha = .85 for males; .83 for females, Calogero et al., 2004; Heinberg & Thompson, 1995; Thompson et al., 1999, 2004).

Internalization-Athlete. Internalization-Athlete that represented internalization of athletic ideals and sports figures in the media was measured with the use of five 5-point scales from 1 ("strongly disagree") to 5 ("strongly agree," Cronbach's alpha = .70 for males; .71 for females, Calogero et al., 2004; Heinberg & Thompson, 1995; Thompson et al., 1999, 2004).

Pressures. Media pressure to achieve certain body size ideals was another variable measured with multiple 5-point items. from 1 ("strongly disagree") to 5 ("strongly agree," Cronbach's alpha = .81 for males; .85 for females, Calogero et al., 2004; Heinberg & Thompson, 1995; Thompson et al., 1999, 2004).

Information. Information was conceptualized as the degree to which media is used as a source of Information for determining body size ideal (Heinberg & Thompson, 1995; Thompson et al. 1999). The variable was measured with nine 5-point items from 1 ("strongly disagree") to 5 ("strongly agree," Cronbach's alpha = .51 for males; .61 for females, Calogero et al., 2004; Heinberg & Thompson, 1995; Thompson et al., 1999, 2004).

Gender. Gender was included in the analysis because it was predicted that viewing television shows would be associated with body image variables in two gender groups differently.

Results

Simple linear and multiple regression tests were run to explore the relationships among independent variables (total TV show viewing; viewing Western TV shows; viewing Arabic TV shows; viewing TV shows with skinny prominent characters; viewing TV shows with characters who have average body types) and dependent measures (Appearance Orientation, Appearance Evaluation, Overweight Preoccupation, Self-Classified Weight, body area satisfaction, General-Internalization, Internalization from watching athletes, Pressure felt from aesthetic ideals, and Information). We focus on the most relevant data.

We ran nine simple linear regressions to explore the association between total TV show viewing and the nine dependent measures. It was indicated that total TV show viewing was positively correlated with Appearance Orientation., $\beta = .14$, $p \leq .05$, Appearance Evaluation, $\beta = .24$, $p \leq .001$, General-Internalization, $\beta = .37$, $p \leq .001$, Pressure, $\beta = .34$, $p \leq .001$, and Information, $\beta = .31$, $p \leq .001$. The standardized regression coefficients are presented in Table 1.

Table 1: Summary of standardized regression coefficients from simple linear regression analyses between total TV viewing and dependent measures

Independent Variables	Dependent Measures				
	Appearance Orientation	Appearance Evaluation	General-Internalization	Pressure	Information
TV Show Viewing	0.14*	0.24***	0.37***	0.34***	0.31***

*p<.05. **p<.01. ***p<.001.

Nine multiple regressions were conducted to test the relationships between viewing Western and Arabic TV shows and nine dependent measures. First, it was found that viewing Western TV shows explained 4% (R^2) of variance in Overweight Preoccupation (β = .20, $p \leq$ .001) when entered to the model by its own, (F(1,208)=8.71, p≤.05). Viewing Arabic TV shows added less than 1% to the variance explained (R^2 change, non-significant (n.s.); F(2,208)=4.48, p≤.05). Viewing Western shows positively contributed to Overweight Preoccupation (β = .19, $p \leq$ .05; β = .04, n.s., respectively). Second, viewing Western TV shows explained 6% (R^2) of variance in Information (β = .25, $p \leq$ .001) when entered to the model by its own, (F(1,207)=13.54, p≤.001). Viewing Arabic TV shows added 5% to the variance explained (R^2 change, p≤.001; F(2,207)=12.68, p≤.001). Viewing both Western and Arabic shows positively contributed to Information (β = .17, $p \leq$ .05; β = .23, $p \leq$ .001, respectively). Third, viewing Western TV shows explained 9% (R^2) of variance in Pressure (β = .29, $p \leq$ .001) when entered to the model by its own, (F(1,207)=19.06, p≤.001). Viewing Arabic TV shows added 1% to the variance explained (R^2 change, p=.87; F(2,207)=11.11, p≤.001). Viewing Western shows positively contributed to Pressure but the same phenomenon was not observed with Arabic shows (β = .25, $p \leq$ .001; β = .12, n.s., respectively). Fourth, viewing Western TV shows explained 11% (R^2) of variance in General-Internalization ((β = .33, $p \leq$ .001)) when entered to the model by its own, (F(1,207)=25.49, p≤.001). Viewing Arabic TV shows added 2% to the variance explained (R^2 change, p≤.05; F(2,207)=14.91, p≤.001). Viewing both Western and Arabic shows positively contributed to General-Internalization (β = .29, p ≤ .001; β = .14, p ≤ .05, respectively). The standardized regression coefficients are presented in Table 2.

Table 2: Overall summary of standardized regression coefficients from multiple regression analyses between viewing Western TV shows, viewing Arabic TV shows and dependent measures

Independent Variables	Dependent Measures			
	Overweight Preoccupation	Information	Pressure	General-Internalization
Western TV Shows	0.19*	0.17*	0.25***	0.29***
Arabic TV Shows	0.04	0.23***	0.12	0.14*

*p<.05 **p<.01 ***p<.001 .

Nine multiple regressions were conducted to test the relationships between viewing Western and Arabic TV shows and nine dependent measures with the sample split by gender, i.e., responses from males and females were analyzed separately.

Males. First, the model with the two TV show viewing variables and Appearance Evaluation as a DV was significant, $F(2,106)=3.42$, p≤.05, with viewing both Western and Arabic shows explaining 6% (R^2) of the variance in Appearance Evaluation although Arabic shows were not statistically significant on this variable (β = .27, n.s.; β = -.19, p =.07, respectively). The more male respondents viewed both types of shows, the less positively they evaluated their appearance. Second, viewing Western TV shows explained 7% (R^2) of variance in Self-Classified Weight (β = .25, p ≤ .05) when entered to the model by its own, ($F(1,106)=7.94$, p≤.05). Viewing Arabic TV shows added only 1% to the variance explained and was not significant (R^2 change, n.s.; $F(2,106)=4.35$, p≤.05). Viewing Western shows positively contributed to Self-Classified Weight, while Arabic shows were not significant in this regard (β = .23, p ≤ .05; β = .09, n.s., respectively). Third, viewing Western TV shows explained 5% (R^2) of variance in General-Internalization (β = .22, p ≤

.05) when entered to the model by its own, (F(1,105)=5.31, p≤.05). Viewing Arabic TV shows added 2% to the variance explained and so was not a significant factor (R^2 change, n.s.; F(2,105)=3.50, p≤.05). Viewing both Western and Arabic shows positively contributed to General-Internalization (β = .17, n.s.; β = .13, n.s., respectively).

Females. First, viewing Western TV shows explained 6% (R^2) of variance in Information (β = .25, $p \leq .05$) when entered to the model by its own, (F(1,96)=6.28, p≤.05). Viewing Arabic TV shows added 8% to the variance explained (R^2 change, p≤.05; F(2,96)=7.99, p≤.001). Viewing both Western and Arabic shows positively contributed to Information (β = .20, $p \leq .05$; β = .29, $p \leq .05$, respectively). Second, viewing Western TV shows explained 6% (R^2) of variance in Pressure (β = .24, $p \leq .05$) when entered to the model by its own, (F(1,96)=5.84, p≤.05). Viewing Arabic TV shows added less than 1% to the variance explained and was not a significant agent (R^2 change, n.s.; F(2,96)=3.14, p≤.05). Viewing Western positively contributed to Pressure with Arabic shows having negligible effect in this area (β = .23, $p \leq .05$; β = .07, n.s., respectively). Third, viewing Western TV shows explained 11% (R^2) of variance in General-Internalization (β = .33, $p \leq .001$) when entered to the model by its own, (F(1,96)=11.46, p≤.001). Viewing Arabic TV shows added 2% to the variance explained and so was not a significant variable (R^2 change, n.s.; F(2,96)=6.95, p≤.05). Viewing both Western shows positively contributed to General-Internalization but Arabic show viewing was not significant (β = .30, $p \leq .05$; β = .15, n.s., respectively). The standardized regression coefficients are presented in Table 3 for males and Table 4 for females:

Table 3: *Males*. A summary of standardized regression coefficients from multiple regression analyses between viewing Western TV shows, viewing Arabic TV shows and dependent measures

Independent Variables	Dependent Measures		
	Appearance Evaluation	Self- Classified Weight	General-Internalization
Western TV Shows	-0.19	0.23*	0.17
Arabic TV Shows	0.27	0.09	0.13

p<.05.

Table 4: *Females*. A summary of standardized regression coefficients from multiple regression analyses between viewing Western TV shows, viewing Arabic TV shows and dependent measures

Independent Variables	Dependent Measures		
	Information	Pressure	General-Internalization
Western TV Shows	0.20*	0.23*	0.30*
Arabic TV Shows	0.29*	0.07	0.15

*p<.05.

Finally, we ran nine multiple regressions separately for male and female respondents to test the relationships between viewing TV shows with skinny prominent characters and viewing TV shows with characters who have average body types as IVs and Appearance Orientation, Appearance Evaluation, Overweight Preoccupation, Self-Classified Weight, Body Areas Satisfaction, General-Internalization, Internalization from watching athletes, Pressure felt from aesthetic ideals, and Information as DVs.

Males. First, viewing TV shows with skinny characters explained 6% (R^2) of variance in Appearance Evaluation (β = -.25, $p \leq .05$) when entered to the model by its own, (F(1,113)=7.57, p≤.05). The model with the two TV show viewing variables (viewing TV shows with skinny characters and viewing TV shows with average body characters) and Appearance Evaluation as a DV was significant, as well, F(2,113)=4.02, p≤.05, with viewing TV shows with average body characters explaining extra .04% (R^2) of the variance in

Appearance Evaluation (β = -.21, p≤.05 for skinny; β = -.08, n.s. for average). The more male respondents viewed both types of shows, but especially shows with skinny characters, the less positively they evaluated their appearance. Second, viewing shows with skinny characters positively contributed to Overweight Preoccupation (β = .19, p ≤ .05), explaining 4% (R^2) of variance in the DV, F(1,113)=4.18, p≤.05. Third, the model with the two TV show viewing variables (viewing TV shows with skinny characters and viewing TV shows with average body characters) and Self-Classified weight as a DV was significant, F(2,113)=4.50, p≤.05, with both IVs explaining 8% (R^2) of the variance in Self-Classified Weight (β =.03, n.s. for skinny; β = .28, p≤.05 for average). Viewing TV shows, especially those with average-body-type characters, was positively associated with Self-Classified Weight. Fourth, viewing shows with skinny characters was positively correlated with Information (β = .20, p ≤ .05), explaining 4% (R^2) of variance in the DV, F(1,112)=4.43, p≤.05. Fifth, viewing shows with skinny characters explained 8% (R^2) of variance in Pressure (β = .29, p ≤ .05) when entered to the model by its own, (F(1,112)=9.32, p≤.05). Viewing shows with average characters added less than 1% to the variance explained (R^2 change, n.s.; F(2,112)=4.66, p≤.05). Viewing both types of shows, but especially, shows with skinny characters, positively contributed to Pressure (β = .26, p ≤ .05 for skinny; β = .03, n.s. for average). Sixth, viewing shows with skinny characters explained 7% (R^2) of variance in General-Internalization (β = .27, p ≤ .05) when entered to the model by its own, (F(1,112)=8.64, p≤.05). Viewing shows with average body characters added less than 1% to the variance explained (R^2 change, n.s.; F(2,112)=4.37, p≤.05). Viewing both types of shows, but especially shows with skinny characters, positively contributed to General-Internalization (β = .25, p ≤ .05 for skinny; β = .04, n.s. for average).

Females. First, viewing shows with skinny characters positively contributed to Overweight Preoccupation (β = .21, p ≤ .05), explaining 4% (R^2) of variance in the DV, F(1,111)=5.12, p≤.05. Second, viewing shows with skinny characters explained 9% (R^2) of variance in Information (β = .30, p ≤ .001) when entered to the model by its own, (F(1,111)=11.25, p≤.001). Viewing shows with average characters added extra 1% to the variance explained (R^2

change, n.s.; $F(2,111)=6.38$, $p \leq .05$). Viewing both types of shows are positively associated with Information ($\beta = .19$, *n.s.* for skinny; $\beta = .16$, *n.s.* for average). Third, viewing shows with skinny characters explained 7% (R^2) of variance in Pressure ($\beta = .27$, $p \leq .05$) when entered to the model by its own, ($F(1,111)=8.74$, $p \leq .05$). Viewing shows with average characters added less than 1% to the variance explained (R^2 change, n.s.; $F(2,111)=4.36$, $p \leq .05$). Viewing both types of shows, but especially, shows with skinny characters, positively contributed to Pressure ($\beta = .25$, $p = .07$ for skinny; $\beta = .03$, *n.s.* for average). Fourth, viewing shows with skinny characters explained 10% (R^2) of variance in General-Internalization ($\beta = .32$, $p \leq .001$) when entered to the model by its own, ($F(1,111)=12.74$, $p \leq .001$). Viewing shows with average body characters added another 3% to the variance explained (R^2 change, $p = .06$; $F(2,111)=8.35$, $p \leq .001$). Viewing both types of shows, but especially shows with average body characters, positively contributed to General-Internalization ($\beta = .14$, *n.s.* for skinny; $\beta = .25$, $p = .06$ for average). The standardized regression coefficients are presented in Table 5 for males and Table 6 for females:

Table 5: *Males.* A summary of standardized regression coefficients from multiple regression analyses between TV shows with Skinny Characters, TV shows with Average Body Characters and dependent measures

Independent Variables	Dependent Measures					
	Appearance Evaluation	Overweight Preoccupation	Self-Classified Weight	Information	Pressure	General-Internalization
TV Shows with Skinny Characters	-0.21*	0.19*	0.03	0.20*	0.26*	0.25*
TV Shows with Average-Body Characters	-0.08	-	0.28*	-	0.03	0.04

*p<.05.

Table 6: *Females.* A summary of standardized regression coefficients from multiple regression analyses between TV shows with Skinny Characters, TV shows with Average Body Characters and dependent measures

Independent Variables	Dependent Measures			
	Overweight Preoccupation	Information	Pressure	General-Internalization
TV Shows with Skinny Characters	0.21*	0.19	0.25	0.14
TV Shows with Average-Body Characters	-	0.16	0.03	0.25

*$p<.05$.

Discussion

The results of our data analyses show that total TV show viewing is positively correlated with Appearance Orientation, Appearance Evaluation, General-Internalization, Pressure, and Information. Corresponding with our hypotheses, the results also showed that the effects of viewing Western TV shows was more significant than the effect of viewing Arabic TV shows when measuring Overweight Preoccupation, Information, Pressure, and General-Internalization.

We can surmise from these results that Media both Arab and Western images positively correlate with how respondents in our sample view their body image. This reinforces our hypotheses that watching TV shows will lead to great body greater Appearance Evaluation. As the adolescents in our study consume TV it appears many are using both western images and Arab images as the barometer of the ideal body type. The biggest impact here is Overweight Preoccupation. Our study finds that Western media images may be eroding the traditional cultural norms of what is considered overweight, with TV shows often depicting thin female models or athletic males. This transmission is also more readily available from Western programs than Arab shows because Arab shows often feature characters dressed in cultural attire, which precludes displaying the body. Furthermore on many variables such as preoccupation, Information Pressure and internalization Western shows are having a greater impact on the body image of the respondents as well. Since in many cases the results of the Western images were more significant than those found from Arab shows such as the pressure to achieve a certain ideal body type, and then we can deduce that by the way of the social comparison theory that the effects of media imperialism on body image are indeed present in our study. It appears in cultures such as Kuwait where there is tendency to view the west as being more progressive and setting trends, that the citizens, especially the youth, are turning to western media images. In countries like these where leisure time and disposable income is high, the population often turns to the west as the trendsetter of where they should be shopping, how they should be dressed, where they should vacation etc. To facilitate this they often turn to TV shows where their favorite characters are clad in the latest designer clothes, drink the latest cocktails and drive the latest trendy car. As Kuwait is a collectivist society with limited individualism, citizens and residents may depend on these characters as an outlet and seek to imitate their way of life. Through the social comparison theory people may be asking *"What I am missing?" "Why don't I have that?"*, or *"Why don't I look like that?"* The Hermes Birkin bag mentioned in an episode of *Sex and the City* can lead to a demand for the item from the women in Kuwait. A car driven on *Top Gear* may cause a backlog on orders of that model from local car dealers because Kuwaitis maybe comparing themselves to west and surmising they themselves are missing something if they don't have what they see on television. Along this line, the body itself is a commodity that these TV shows are explicitly or implicitly selling to the audiences in Kuwait. Western images now represent the archetype of beauty, thinness and athleticism.

Western and Arabic shows:
Males:

When looking at the effects of viewing western and Arabic TV shows on male body image evaluation; the results showed that the more male respondents viewed both types of shows, the less positively they evaluated their appearance. In addition, viewing both Western and Arabic shows positively contributed to Self-Classified Weight and to General-Internalization. Once again, we are seeing the impact of the social comparison theory. The males in our sample are gauging themselves based on the images they see on TV. There is a direct comparison not only with Arab characters but through the impact of media imperialism, these males are also assessing their bodies based on western standards of masculinity and male beauty. It appears that the males are internalizing images they consume and are thinking about their bodies in comparison to what they see. The males are then routinely not happy with their body types after making this comparison.

Females:

As for females, viewing both Western and Arabic shows positively contributed to Information, Pressure and General-Internalization. Differently from their male counterparts females in our sample are specifically seeking out television programs as a way to gather Information on their bodies. This process of Information gathering led many of the women in the study to feel the pressure to conform to these body type standards. So while the men were unhappy with their weight and thought about their bodies, in keeping with our hypotheses on gender differences and the expectancy of greater negative effects of media imperialism on females, the women in our study appear more susceptible to media images and often times seek out Information and social comparison. Females then customarily felt the pressure to conform to these ideals more so than the men did.

Skinny and average shows:
Males:

The data analyzed also revealed that the more male respondents viewed TV shows depicting skinny and average characters, but especially shows with skinny characters, the less positively they evaluated their appearance. Second, viewing shows with skinny characters positively contributed to Overweight Preoccupation. Viewing TV shows, especially those with average-body-type characters, was positively associated with Self-Classified Weight. Fourth, viewing shows with skinny characters was positively correlated with Information. Unlike what was found when we analyzed the results based on show type: Arab and Western shows, when we divided the data by body type (skinny and average) and looked at 'Information', males exhibited similar patterns to the females. They too were watching shows and seeking out information on bodies. Viewing both types of shows, but especially, shows with skinny characters, positively contributed to Pressure. Viewing both types of shows, but especially shows with skinny characters, positively contributed to General-Internalization in males surveyed. By breaking down our results by dominant body types portrayed on TV programs, we are better able to understand why and when men are thinking more about their bodies. When shows depicted skinny characters the men were generally unhappy with their weight, demonstrating that the specific type of character and TV program depicting a predominate skinny body type was likely to lead to men feeling negative about their bodies while average characters only led men to think about their physiques but not necessarily to critique it. This reinforces our hypotheses that consuming programs depicting skinny characters would lead to body dissatisfaction. In addition, both physique types demonstrate a clear use of social comparison to assess and judge one's own form.

Females:

As predicted, viewing shows with skinny characters positively contributed to Overweight Preoccupation. Viewing both types of shows (depicting skinny and average characters) are positively associated with Information. Viewing both types of shows, but especially, shows with skinny characters, positively contributed to Pressure. What we found was that viewing both types of shows, but especially shows with average body characters, positively contributed to General-Internalization. What is profound is that it is average body types lead to internalization and not shows with predominately-skinny characters, something we did not expect to find in our data but it does highlight our argument that women would be more affected by social comparison and media imperialism than men. It is hard to determine what the females are thinking and why they are internalizing when viewing shows with average characters, perhaps some are able to make sense of the idea that the standard of beauty is not only those depicting thin model-like characters but that women with average bodies. Conversely, they could just be wondering why the women with average bodies don't feel ashamed or embarrassed that their body types are not ideal and this may lead to the female respondents scrutinizing their own appearance.

Limitations and future research

Our study examined and found significant results on the effects of mediated body images on adolescents living in Kuwait. We were able to demonstrate that young adults were comparing their bodies to the images they saw in both western and Arabic media and this was leading to body dissatisfaction. Furthermore, our study showed significant effects of Western media imperialism on the effects of body image on our respondents. However, our study did not examine how particular TV characters affected this dynamic. It could be theorized that forming bonds with a character leads to greater Appearance Evaluation and body dissatisfaction. For example, if a female idealized Jennifer Anniston on the TV show *Friends,* would this lead to greater body dissatisfaction than watching the contestants on *America's Next Top Model* to whom she may have no attachment? Furthermore, our study leaves open room to present media messages (television shows) to the respondents before surveying their dissatisfaction with their bodies, rather than relying on their recollection of TV consumption. Moreover, due to the high socio-economic status of our sample, many may be consuming more media than their western counterparts due to a large amount of leisure time and less social activities available in Kuwait than in the West. Future research could control and segment respondents by amount of hours spent in an average week consuming media, especially TV. In addition, inquiry could be made on what percentage of disposable income is being spent on improving body image. And lastly, further research could control for external variables such as peer pressure and parental messages on body image.

References

Agliata, D., & Tantleff-Dunn, S. (2004). The impact of media exposure on males' body image. *Journal of Social and Clinical Psychology*, 23 ed., Vol. 1, (pp. 7-22).

Al-Subaie, A. S. (2000). Some correlates of dieting Behavior in Saudi schoolgirls. *International Journal of Eating Disorders*, 28, (pp. 242–246).

Anschutz, D. J., Van Strien, T., & Engels, R. (2011). Exposure to slim Images in mass media: television commercials as reminders of restriction in restrained Eaters. *Health Psychology*, 2008 (July), Vol. 27 (4), (pp. 401-408).

Arab Advisors Group. (2007). *94.2% of Households in Kuwait have Sat TV receivers*. http://www.arabadvisors.com/Pressers/presser-071107.htm. Accessed March 4, 2014.

Cash, T. (2000). Multidimensional Body-Self Relations Questionnaire: MBSRQ user's manual. Norfolk, VA: Old Dominion University.

Cash, T. F., Winstead, B. A., & Janda, J. H. (1985). Your body, yourself: a reader survey. Psychology Today, 19 (7), (pp. 22–26).

Cash, T. F., Winstead, B. A., & Janda, J. H. (1986). Body image survey report: The great American shape-up. Psychology Today, 20 (4), (pp 30–44).

Chronister, K. M., Forrest, L., Lau, A. S. M., & Lum, S. K. (2006). Asian American college women's body image: a pilot study. *Cultural Diversity and Ethnic Minority Psychology*, 12 ed., Vol. 2, (pp. 259-274).

CIA. *The World Fact book*, (Kuwait). https://www.cia.gov/library/publications/the-world-factbook/geos/ku.html. Accessed March 4, 2014.

Dominick, Joseph, R (2009). *The Dynamics of Mass Communication: Media in the Digital Age*. New York, NY: McGraw-Hill

Farquhar, J. C., & Wasylkiw, L. (2007). Media images of men: trends and consequences of body conceptualization. 8 ed., Vol. 3, (pp. 145-160). *Psychology of Men & Masculinity.*

Fedorak, Shirley A. (2008). *Anthropology matters.* Toronto, Canada: Higher Education University of Toronto Press

Fejes, F. (1981). Media imperialism: An Assessment. *Media, culture & society, 3,* 281-289. Retrieved from: http://courses.essex.ac.uk/gv/gv905/W05 Readings/fejes_media_imperialism.pdf

Fister, S. M., & Smith, G. T. (2004). Media effects on expectancies: exposure to realistic female images as a protective factor. *Psychology of Addictive Behavior,* 18 ed., Vol. 4, (pp. 394-397).

Frisby, Cynthia M. (2004). Does race matter? effects of idealized images on African American women's perceptions of body esteem, *journal of black studies.* Vol. 34, No. 3 (pp. 323-347).

Grabe, S., Ward, L. M., & Hyde, J. S. (2008). The Role of The Media In Body Image Concerns Among Women: A Meta-Analysis Of Experimental and Correlational Studies. (134 ed., Vol. 3, (pp. 460-476). *Psychological Bulletin.*

Hargreaves, D. A., & Tiggerman, M. (2009). Muscular ideal media images and men's body image: social comparison processing and individual vulnerability. *Psychology of Men & Masculinity,* 10 ed., Vol. 2,(pp. 109-119).

Harrison, K. (1997). Does interpersonal attraction to thin media personalities promote eating disorders? *Journal of Broadcasting and Electronic Media, 41* (pp. 478–500).

Harrison, K. (2000). The body electric: thin-ideal media. *Journal of Communication,* (pp. 119-143).

Heinberg, L. J., Thompson, J. K. (1995). Development and validation of the sociocultural attitudes towards appearance questionnaire (SATAQ). *International Journal of Eating Disorders, 17,* (pp. 81-89).

Hobza, C. L., Peugh, J. L., Walker, K. E., & Yakushko, O. (2007). What about men? social comparison and the effects of media images on body and self-esteem. *Psychology of Men & Masculinity.* 8 ed., Vol. 3, (pp. 161-172).

Hopkins, C., Morrison, M. A., & Morrison, T. G. (2003). Striving for bodily perfection? an exploration of the drive for muscularity in Canadian men. 4th ed., Vol. 2,. *Psychology of Men & Masculinity,* (pp. 111-120).

International Telecommunication Union. (2011). *Individuals using the Internet,* (2000-2011-1) Accessed on March 4, 2014.

Morry, M. M., & Staska, S. L. (2001). Magazine exposure: internalization, self-objectification, eating attitudes, and body satisfaction in male and female university students. *Canadian Psychological Association,* 33 ed., Vol. 4, (pp. 269-279)

Petras, James. (1994). Cultural imperialism in late 20th century. E*conomic and Political Weekly,* Vol. 29, No. 32 (Aug. 6, 1994), (pp. 2070-2073). Retrieved from JSTOR database.

Pressreference.com. http://www.pressreference.com/Gu-Ku/Kuwait.html. Accessed March 3, 2014

Suls, Jerry, Martin, René, Wheeler, Ladd. (Oct., 2002). Social comparison: why, with whom, and with what effect? *Current Directions in Psychological Science,* Vol. 11, No. 5., (pp. 159-163) Sage Publications, Inc. Association for Psychological Science retrieved from JSTOR database.

Soh, N. L., Touyz, S. W. and Surgenor, L. J. (2006). Eating and body Image disturbances across cultures: a review. *European Eating Disorders Review*, 14, (pp. 54–65). doi: 10.1002/erv.678

Stice, E., Schupak-Neuberg, E., Shaw, H. E., & Stein, R. I. (1994). Relation of media exposure to eating disorder symptomatology: An examination of mediating mechanisms. *American Psychological Association,* 103 ed., Vol. 4, (pp. 836-840).

Thomas J., Khan S., Abdulrahman A.A. (2010). Eating attitudes and Body Image Concerns Among Female University Students in the United Arab Emirates. *Appetite,* 54 (3), (pp. 595-598).

Thompson, J. K., Heinberg, L. J., Altabe, M. N., & Tantleff-Dunn, S. (1999). Exacting beauty: Theory, assessment, and treatment of body image disturbance. Washington DC: American Psychological Association.

Thornton, B., & Moore, S. (1993). Physical attractiveness contrast effect: Implications for self-esteem and evaluations of the social self. *Personality and Social Psychology Bulletin, 19*, (pp. 474–480).

Wheeler, D. (2000). New Media, Globalization and Kuwaiti National Identity. *Middle East Journal,* Vol. 54, No. 3. (pp. 432-444). Retrieved from JSTOR database.

Wykes, M., & Gunter, B. (2005). The media and body image, *Culture & Society*, Vol. 29, No. 2, (pp. 357-358).

As published in the Construction of Social Psychology book –Ch 10– Pages 105-121.

Attachment Styles and Parasocial Relationships: A Collectivist Society Perspective

Juliet Dinkha[1], Charles Mitchell[2] & Mourad Dakhli[3]
[1]*American University of Kuwait, Kuwait,*
[2]*Independent Researcher & communications consultant, Kuwait*
[3]*Georgia State University, USA*

Abstract

In this study we investigate parasocial relationships in media; more specifically we explore why audience members fashion attachments with television personalities. The study aligns with previous research in the area by Cole and Leets (1999) that looked at attachments formed with media figures and the correlation to level of attachments in real-life relationships. In their study, Cole and Leets (1999) used a three-dimensional attachment scale that included anxious-ambivalent, avoidant, and secure, and found those with higher insecurity or unstable real-life relationships have stronger parasocial relationships. We surveyed university age respondents and we used the same scales as Cole and Leets (1999) to examine whether in Kuwait, where dating violates social norms and looser bonds are found outside of the home, that stronger parasocial relationships with media personalities will be found because of the need to fulfill relationship needs outside of family. Our hypotheses in this chapter is that higher levels of anxious-ambivalents and avoidants both will be found due to the strict collectivist nature of the society forcing many to compensate for lack of real world relationships by forming mediated bonds. Moreover, we posited and discovered that that these two groups also showed the highest levels of parasocial relationships in our sample.

Keywords: parasocial, attachment styles, Kuwait, collectivism, media.

1. Introduction

This study proposes to investigate how parasocial relationships in media are formed in a traditional collectivist society like Kuwait and how they are affected by attachments found in real world relationships. We chose Kuwait for this study as it is seen as a highly collectivist (Hofstede, 2001), conservative society that provides a maximally different context from that of the United States and the West where most parasocial relationship studies were conducted (Bond & Calvert, 2014; Cohen, 2004; Cohen, 1997, Cole &Leets, 1999; Dibble, Hartmann, & Rosaen, 2015; Eyal & Cohen, 2006; Hazan & Shaver, 1987; Rizzo, 2005; Rubin, Perse, & Powell, 1985; Woodley & Movius, 2012). A Parasocial Relationship (PSR) is defined as a one-sided relationship that an audience member fashions with a television personality (Bond & Calvert, 2014; Cohen, 2004; Cohen, 1997, 1999; Eyal & Cohen, 2006). Part of the schema of a PSR is loyalty to a given television program manifested in regularly viewing of a show. The term parasocial relationship was originally coined in Horton and Wohl (1956) where they describe it as a "seeming face-to-face relationship" (p. 215).

The date of the study might delineate the definition of face-to-face. At that time the researchers used television personalities like Steve Allen and Liberace to help define the type of persona the audience seeks when establishing a bond with a celebrity. In the era of Horton and Wohl, the PSRs perused were often ones where the personality spoke directly to the television and the studio audiences, creating an illusion that the PSR was reciprocal and thus creating a greater sense of intimacy. This can in fact be compared to modern day talk show programs. For example, the widely popular television show *Oprah Winfrey* has some of the same attributes described in the Horton study of the *Steve Allen Show*. Winfrey has often addressed the home audience as if she were speaking directly with them (Horton & Wohl, 1956; Woodley & Movius, 2012, Dibble et al., 2015). Lewis (2000) expressed this idea as "The line separating the persona and the audience is further blurred if the media character steps out of the particular format of the show and literally blends with the studio audience" (p. 12).

Talking to the screen through close-ups such as Winfrey does provides a human-side to the performer and engages the TV viewers just as it does the studio audience, thus giving the impression that the performer is a regular person and so solidifying the PSR (Lewis, 2000). Addressing the audiences directly is also something that is quite prevalent in children's programming, with many of those characters being scripted to speak directly to young children in the viewing audience (Bond & Calvert, 2014). In fact, it isn't just about adults; Bond & Calvert (2014) noted that the children as young as 21 months old can develop strong parasocial relationships. So the phenomenon of parasocial ties is not something exclusive to older audiences only. Correspondingly, children were able to make bonds with anthropomorphic characters such as puppets and cartoon characters with reinforcement of the relationship taking place with toys, parental encouragement and repeated exposure to those characters.

Researchers have suggested that viewers, including children, form strong PSRs as a result of the perceived realism of the program and also due to the realism of the characters and the physical and social attractiveness of these personalities (Bond & Calvert, 2014; Camella, 2001; Eyal & Cohen, 2006). It is believed that the viewer suspends disbeliefs about the fictionalization of the television characters even when they know that the television program is scripted as is the case for many talk shows, live programs, and so-called reality shows. Our study aims to look at the impact of these relationships in a collectivist society such as Kuwait and to examine how these relationships are impacted by certain attachment types as described in section 2.1 of our literature review.

2. Background

It is quite often the most socially popular or desirable characters who become the subject of PSRs for the dedicated audience (Bond & Calvert, 2014). Eyal and Cohen (2006) examined this phenomenon through the highly popular show *Friends*. 'Rachel' an attractive character on the program was rated as the most popular and was ranked as the person with whom the majority of those surveyed formed a bond. 'Ross' on the other hand, was rated as the least popular character and who had the least amount of associated PSRs. Other factors that were found to contribute to the strength of PSRs include shared values, background similarity, identification and communication styles, and perceived homophily with the character (Bryant & Oliver, 2009; Eyal & Cohen, 2006; Slade, Narro & Buchanan, 2014; Manusov & Harvey, 2001). Shared values, identification and predictability help to reinforce the bond to the TV persona and create a sense of empathy whereby the viewer wishes nothing but success and happiness for the character, as if they were personally invested or had some obligation to their favorite star (Lewis, 2000).

Some audience members even come to the conclusion that they know their TV personality as well as they know their own friends. Deep knowledge of a favorite character would generally not be shared among casual viewers of the program. Additionally, a committed fan will generally believe that his or her knowledge of their favorite TV star or celebrity is more expansive than that of a casual viewer or fan. This knowledge would not just be limited to a character's traits, but could also include voice, dress and appearance (Bond & Calvert, 2014; Horton & Wohl, 1956).

Another aspect of the bond of the PSR is the belief that the performer or character would fit neatly into one's social circles (Lewis, 2000). Cole & Leets (1999) describes parasocial relationships as closer than acquaintances, but further than friends or family. This idea came to be referred to as a 'quasi-friendship'. This quasi-friendship is to a certain extent built on the predictability of the character. Just as the audience may know how friends and family would react and behave in a given scenario, so is the case for the TV star. In a scripted show, the characters can be more formulaic than those in real life. Consequently, a TV friend is often more predictable than a close associate in the real world (Horton & Wohl, 1956). In fact, it is found that the strength of the PSR will increase as the audience member is better able to predict the behavior of a given TV personality (Cole & Leets, 1999). This can, in turn, lead to an increased feeling of intimacy within the PSR, an occurrence that was previously described: "They know such a persona in somewhat the same way they know their chosen friend: through direct observation and interpretation of his appearances his gestures and voice, his conversation and conduct in a variety of situations" (Horton & Wohl, 1956, p. 216).

Eyal and Cohen (2006) concluded that PSRs are a strong part of social relationships of many TV viewers with some reporting idolizing and admiring their favorite TV personality (Camella, 2001). Early research has even found little differences in terms of psychological rewards between real world interpersonal relationships and PSRs (Lewis, 2000). However, in general, PSRs do not replace relationships audience members have with friends or family.

Furthermore, the PSR does not discontinue once the program has ended for the week but is a long term relationship that continues beyond the broadcast (Dibble et al., 2015). There are other outlets that allow the audience member to continue the one-sided relationship. There are entire industries around stars and celebrities that help fans immerse into their PSRs. These include press agents, entertainment shows and magazines (Horton & Wohl, 1956). This is further reinforced through the Internet where fans have dedicated websites for their favorite stars, and media outlets and networks establish official websites and social media pages for the shows and their many characters. These sites are full of interactive options such as e-mails, chats, blogs, and so forth. Americanidol.com for example, allows fans of the hit reality show to view behind the scene photographs from the latest episodes, peruse biographies of contestants, and discuss and vote for their favorite singer. Reality shows like *American Idol* and *So You Think You Can Dance*, go further than other variety programming by asking the audience to shape the content of the program and thusly the future of their PSRs, by voting to keep contestants 'alive' or to vote them off.

The actor himself may be a part of the PSR strengthening process through appearances in talk show programs, interviews in magazines and personal appearances at award shows. The audience members thus develop a greater sense of closeness to the persona and a stronger belief that they know more about the star, bringing the PSR even closer (Cohen, 2004).

The viewer also has also an important role to fill as a loyal viewer of the show by keeping up with events affecting a favorite TV personality and by not attempting to form bonds with a program that may be out of his or her intellectual reach such as the example of a child forming bonds with a persona in an adult show, or vice versa (Horton & Wohl, 1956).

Some viewers are said to use mediated relationships as a substitute for interpersonal ones based on a fantasy provided by a given TV character where they experience achievement vicariously through the character's TV experiences. Consequently, the TV personality becomes more than a quasi-friend, but rather a role model emulated by his dedicated fan (Horton & Wohl, 1956). This is best depicted through the PSRs formed with famous rock stars that go to great lengths to present a glamorous, hedonistic life though their music videos and on the concert stage.

In developing and sustaining mediated bonds, many viewers tend to surrender to the experiences of the characters in the fictional situation presented in the program rather than attempting to theorize how they would handle the situation themselves. Therefore, and in this respect, the PSRs serve an escapist role (Eyal & Rubin, 2003). Though given that the PSR is to a large extent based on attractiveness and homophily, it would be reasonable to assume that the viewer may act similarly in an analogous circumstance.

An important question for inquiry is why do some audience members form parasocial relationships while others do not? Cohen (1997) reports that some people use PSRs as a substitution for a lack of interpersonal relationships or as a result of insecurity in their romantic relations. Some studies have found that forming PSRs can help battle loneliness (Adam & Sizemore, 2013). However, subsequent research has cast serious doubts on these propositions. Both Rubin et al (1985) and Cohen (1997) found no correlation between loneliness and the degree to which an audience member fashions PSRs (Cohen 1997; Cole & Leets, 1999; Rubin et al., 1985). Contrary to this compensation argument, it was found that many in secure relationships, especially women, fashion strong PSRs and could use these ties as extensions of their romantic relationships (Adam & Sizemore, 2013). Adam and Sizemore (2013) described scenarios where audience members fashioned romantic parasocial relationships with media characters including strong viewer romantic-based PSRs to characters in the film franchise *Twilight*. Along this line, Cohen (2004) has even suggested that in general the same skills required in sustaining real-world relationships are needed to sustain PSRs.

PSRs have also been found to be dependent on the viewer's gender. While females showed no preferences in the types of personalities they fashion PSRs with, men showed a preference for forming bonds with newscasters first, followed by talk show hosts, and then by sitcom stars (Lewis, 2000). In general, women formed stronger PSRs than men, and reported higher attachment levels, which can lead to a feeling of loss when a TV show is cancelled and a favorite TV character ceases to exist (Eyal & Cohen, 2006).

Self-esteem is another variable that was investigated in the context of PSRs. Self-esteem was not found to be a strong predictor in establishing PSRs, and people with high PSRs were not found to exhibit low self-esteem. Interestingly however, those with high self-esteem tended to form attachments to comedians (Cohen, 2004).

One of the most significant aspects of PSRs is that they effectively illustrate the extent to which media can influence opinions of the audience (Baldwin, Perry & Moffitt, 2004). In one study, the influence on homophobia after forming PSRs with gay male characters was investigated. Studies have shown that a significant reduction in negative attitudes toward homosexuals whether coworkers, friends or classmates was observed when a heterosexual forms PSRs with homosexual characters or celebrities.

While a large body of research has focused on PSRs and television, a number of scholars have looked at other areas. For example, Burnett and Beto (2000) examined PSRs in the context of romance novels. The results were in general similar to what was found in television-related PSRs. The writing style of the novel was found to be a factor in the way PSRs were established. For instance, an emphasis on the attractiveness of a given character is a paramount editorial rule in romance novels. Attractiveness is one of the key components that studies have listed as desirable to the viewer when forming a TV or film-based PSR (Adam & Sizemore, 2013). Women, in particular, identified with, and established stronger bonds to female characters. Many in fact felt that they empathized greatly with their favorite literary heroine and expressed sadness when the book ended (Burnett & Beto, 2000).

2.1. Attachment and Parasocial Relationships

Cole and Leets (1999) support the proposition that a key a predictor of forming PSRs is the level of attachment in interpersonal relationships. The way in which a person engages and forms attachments in adult relationships originates in the relationship the person had with their primary caregiver(s) as a child, generally the mother. Children are said to go through various stages of separation from their caregiver that include protest, despair and detachment (Hazan & Shaver, 1987; Konishi & Hymel, 2014; Nathanson & Manohar, 2012). Based on research, a caregiver who is overly critical and withdrawn or rejects their child would normally produce an adult classified as an avoidant. A caregiver who is inconsistent with her child, consoling them when they cry, but sometimes not interfering, would produce an adult who is anxious-ambivalent. Finally, caregivers who are consistent with the child would raise a secure adult (Hazan & Shaver, 1987; Konishi & Hymel, 2014; Nathanson & Manohar, 2012).

Hazan and Shaver (1987) theorized the personality types identified in their study could predict adult romantic love behavior. In their study, 620 respondents were asked how they felt about their interpersonal and romantic relationships. Their dating status was also surveyed, including the length of the current or last relationship. Their survey also included information on childhood experiences, degree and type of attachment to the mother and the father, as well as the nature of the relationship between the two parents. No differences were found in attachment styles among respondents who had parents who were divorced as children and those who didn't, or even among those who had long-term separation from their parents and those who did not. In fact, the key indicator of attachment style found was the quality of the relationship with each parent, while the only gender-related difference noted was that respondents tended to judge their opposite-sex parent more kindly.

What researchers also found was that those who fit the classification of secure had longer lasting relationships than other personality types, and were characterized as happy and trusting. Furthermore, secure adults also reported they could accept their partners' character flaws. Those categorized as avoidants on the other hand had a fear of intimacy, had rocky relationships that lasted on average half as long as those maintained by secures. Lastly, anxious-ambivalents described relationships based on obsession and sexual attraction and like avoidants, experienced relationships that were full of highs and lows (Hazan & Shaver, 1987; Nathanson & Manohar, 2012).

In general, secure respondents saw people as kind-natured and believed that they themselves were persons easy to get along with and were generally liked by others . Anxious-ambivalents described themselves as misunderstood, underappreciated and found it hard to find a partner who would commit to a lasting relationship. Most avoidants reported that they could get along better alone and that one has to be cautious when it comes to interacting with others (Hazan & Shaver, 1987).

Additionally, secure respondents tended to feel secure in their interpersonal relationships and were seen as more trustworthy and were more inclined to maintain stable relationships. Avoidant types tended to avoid relationships, especially the romantic ones, and found it harder to socialize. They also held mostly negative attitudes toward relationships and were increasingly upset when relationships ended. Anxious-ambivalent respondents had negative attitudes about themselves and were insecure in their relationships and had high levels of anxiety about abandonment, but nonetheless they reported a strong need to be loved. Anxious-ambivalent respondents tended to also fall in love more easily and more often, and were more likely to be jealous and appeasing during tensions in the relationship (Cohen, 1997; Cole & Leets, 1999).

The three types of attachment styles described above were found to be strong predictors of the depth and nuances of PSRs. For example, anxious-ambivalents were most likely to form PSRs. This was explained by the fact that anxious-ambivalents may find comfort in the stability of their favorite TV personality or celebrity (Cohen, 1997, Cole & Leets, 1999). Correspondingly, homophily was not found to be an indicator in the PSRs of anxious-ambivalents as many anxious-ambivalents formed bonds with stable-type personalities. The same study found avoidants to be the group least likely to fashion PSRs something that parallels their attitudes toward real life relationships. Secure individuals had moderate ties to TV personalities, often forming stronger bonds when they were in a relationship with someone they did not trust. In this case, the stability of a trustworthy TV character may serve a compensatory role for an unstable real-life relationship. Finally, avoidants were unlikely to fashion PSRs even when their own real-life relationships were unstable. This was explained by the fact that avoidants may have given-up on relationships and felt that even media-based relationships left little room for trust (Cole & Leets, 1999).

Attachment styles were also found to play a large role in the depth of the PSRs. Attachments styles can indicate and shape the audiences' feelings and in turn the nature of the bonds with a favorite TV personality. Just like real-world relationships, PSRs may fulfill existing attachment needs (Cohen, 2004; Cole & Leets, 1999; Rubin et al., 1985).

Cohen (2004) and Eyal and Cohen (2006) investigated this area. Cohen (2004) for example, used the final episode of *Friends* and looked at what happens when the PSR comes to an end. He theorized that those with secure attachments would react with less intensity to the end of a PSR. Anxious-ambivalents would have the most adverse reaction to the ending of a PSR, and finally avoidants would have difficulty coping afterwards. The length of the parasocial relationship could also predict the level of difficulty in dealing with the loss as time tends to strengthen relationships. Just as theorized, it was found that anxious-ambivalents faced the greatest difficulty in dealing and coping with the loss of a PSR. This is supported by the fact that

that anxious-ambivalents are more likely to be susceptible to intense anxiety when real world ties end. Interestingly, neither gender nor current relationship status predicted reaction to the end of a PSR. However, contrary to what was suggested by Cohen, there were no significant differences between secures and avoidants in how they reacted to the loss of the PSR, with both groups reporting low anxiety when their PSRs ended (Cohen, 2004).

Cohen's (2003) self-report study measured and assessed reactions of teens and adults, both males and females to the dissolution of their parasocial relationships. Cohen (2003) hypothesis matched his conclusion, that women have stronger parasocial bonds and a breakup is equally as difficult for men as for women.

2.2. Attachment, Parasocial Relationships and Culture

That culture sanctions and determines, or at the very least affects social interaction is a well-established fact in the social sciences literature and has been the focus of numerous discourse and research. From the earliest work of Freud on the internalization of social moral values, and Parsons and Shils' (1951) theory of action, to the more recent work of Triandis (1995, 2001) in the area of cross-cultural social psychology, the important role of the cultural context in shaping how people perceive, react, and interact with others is well recognized. For example, in his formulation of social exchange theory, (Blau, 1964; Cropanzano & Mitchell, 2005; Wikhamn & Hall, 2012) argued that the social context in which exchange takes place defines the rules and guidelines governing exchange and determines the value of what is exchanged as well as the social status of exchange partners and reciprocity. Hofstede (1980), in his large study of work-related values, has found significant differences across cultures in the way people work, interact and respond to organizational processes.

Our study is anchored in the understanding of the importance of culture for interpersonal and parasocial relationships. In particular, we focus on collectivism, and for the attachment styles, we use the three types considered in

Cole and Leets (1999), namely, secure, anxious-ambivalents and avoidants.

Levels of attachment and reaction to separation, autonomy and commitment, interdependence and independence are some of the characteristics that determine a collectivist versus individualistic social cohesion (James & Gilliland, 2013; Kagitcibasi, 1994; Petrakis, 2014; Triandis, 1995).

In collectivist societies, the family unit is based on commitment, attachment and interdependence. The family meets the social needs of the individuals in the group, which helps form a sense of identity, commitment and belonging. Alternatively, in an individualist setting, the emphasis is on the individual, his/her identity, achievement, and independence (James & Gilliland, 2013; Hofstede, 1991; Petrakis, 2014; Pyke & Bengtson, 1996; Triandis, 1995).

In their research on young Adults Attachment Styles, You and Malley-Morrison (2000) compared attachment types in a sample of Caucasian Americans and a sample of collectivist Koreans. They found high amounts of preoccupied attachment styles in the Korean sample that were characterized as having high levels of feelings of unworthiness and greater emphasis on valuing others rather than the self. In a similar study of relationships of Korean students and American students, the former reported less intimate friendships than those found in the American sample (You & Malley-Morrison, 2000). The Korean students in this research reported a preoccupied attachment style where others were seen as untrustworthy and thus the subject felt the need to protect themselves others. The authors note that being from a collectivist society one would expect to find higher levels of trust and attachment to the family. However, this level of closeness did not cover friends or peers, which is contrary to what was found in the American sample. The results of the research are explained by the in-group/out-group distinction that characterizes collectivist societies where high levels of attachment and trust are familial traits and are social experiences not to be shared with outsiders and can be traits inherent to closed societies where people seldom form bonds with those outside the group, family or community (Dakhli, Khorram & Vora, 2007; Earley, 1994; Erez & Earley, 1993; Marková & Gillespie, 2008; Yamagishi, 2011).

These results were further validated by the Schmitt, et al., (2004) study that was conducted with researchers across 62 countries. In this large cross-cultural investigation, student samples from Asia, South America, Western Nations, the Middle East, and Africa were included. Researchers discovered that secure attachment was the most widely reported type with 79% of the cultures in the sample reporting this attachment style as the most prevalent. However, in the collectivist cultures of East Asia, the preoccupied attachment was especially high and this attachment style was also present in the East African cultures. The authors of the study attributed these differences to the predominance of preoccupied attachment (insecure) in collectivist cultures.

Hypotheses

Hypothesis 1. The number of reported anxious-ambivalents and avoidants will be higher in the Kuwaiti sample than in the North American sample.

Hypothesis 2. The degree of parasocial relationships will be higher for anxious-ambivalent and avoidants in Kuwait than reported in the North American sample.

3. Method

i. *Participants*

We collected data from 259 undergraduate students at a private English-language university in Kuwait. About 40% of respondents were males and the rest were 60% females, and about 90% of all respondents were aged 18-23. About 71% of respondents were single, 23% were in a relationship, and only 6% reported being married. With regards to nationality, about 70% of all respondents were Kuwaiti nationals, and the rest were non-nationals.

ii. *Procedure*

Before we distributed our surveys we first pretested by randomly distributing 100 surveys to students and we found no problems with responses. We then made use of research assistants and faculty to distribute the survey at the same private English undergraduate university in Kuwait. The sample consisted of undergraduates, and the anonymous survey was randomly disseminated in classrooms in freshmen, sophomore, junior and senior level courses. We first distributed the parasocial study followed by the attachment survey. The surveys were anonymous as participants were instructed not to fill in any information including their names that would identify them but were asked to fill out standard demographic questions such as age, nationality and gender. Participants were given up to 20 minutes to complete each survey.

iii. *Questionnaire Construction*

To test our hypotheses, we use a survey methodology. We used similar survey items employed by Auter (1992) and Rubin et al. (1985) Table 1 and Feeney and Noller (1992) Table 2. The questions on the parasocial scale (Table 1.) solicit information regarding the nature of a TV viewer's attachment to their favorite TV star and the second survey (Table 2) asked questions to discern attachment style identifying the three types described in our literature review. The 21 items on the parasocial scale ascertained if a parasocial relationship exists and the depth of the parasocial relationship. Samples items include: "My favorite TV star makes me feel comfortable, as if I am with a friend," "I idolize/look up to my favorite TV star," and "I like to compare my ideas with what my favorite TV star says." For the attachment survey we employed a 20-item scale, which measures levels of attachment, namely security versus insecurity; examples include, "My partner often wants me to be more intimate than I feel comfortable being," "I find that others are reluctant to get as close as I would," and "I often worry that my partner won't want to stay with me." Our objective was to compare our results to research done in the western world as described in our literature review (Cohen, 2004; Cohen, 1997, Eyal & Cohen, 2006; Hazan & Shaver, 1987; Rubin et al., 1985) while using the methodology in Cole & Leets (1999) as a principal guide because the authors in the latter study tested the relationship between parasocial relationships and attachment styles specifically in their research. We did not add or change questions in either survey because the surveys were culturally neutral and can be applied to Kuwait because questions were not western-specific.

iv. *Parasocial Interaction*

In their seminal research Rubin et al. (1985) employed parasocial interaction scale, which was used to gauge the respondents bond with their favorite TV star (Auter, 1992). The scale that was used consisted of 20-items. We replaced 'newscaster' used in the original survey from Auter and followed the scale variation employed by Cole and Leets (1999), which just used the term 'TV personality'. In line with Cole and Leets (1999), we utilized an open-ended question asking participants to identify their favorite TV personality (Q.21). The items in our scale were measured using a 5-point Likert scale where 1 represented strongly disagree and 5 represented strongly agree. The unidimensional scale displayed similar reliability in both cultures collectivist and individualistic (see Table 1.).

	Table 1. Parasocial Interaction Scale Items (adapted from Auter, 1992; Rubin et al., 1985)	
		Unidimensional Factor Loading
7.	My favorite TV star (person) makes me feel comfortable, as if I am with friends.	0.658
11.	I look forward to watching my favorite TV star's show.	0.647
5.	When I'm watching my favorite TV star (person), I feel as if I am part of the group.	0.633
12.	If my favorite TV star (person) appeared on another television program, I would watch the program.	0.623
10.	Watching my favorite TV star (person) makes me feel less lonely.	0.599
15.	If there were a story about my favorite TV star (person) in a newspaper or magazine, I would read it.	0.547
17.	I would like to meet my favorite TV star in person.	0.545
19.	I find my favorite TV star (person) to be attractive.	0.535
13.	My favorite TV star (person) and I seem to have a lot in common.	0.531
20.	I am not as satisfied when other characters replace or overshadow my favorite TV star (person).	0.52
21.	I idolize/look up to my favorite TV star (person)	0.519
6.	I like to compare my ideas with what my favorite TV star (person) says.	0.509
18.	I think my favorite TV star (person) is like an old friend.	0.508

16.	I miss seeing my favorite TV star (person) when his or her program is no longer on TV.	0.506
9.	I like hearing the voice of my favorite TV star (person) in my home.	0.503
3.	When my favorite TV star (person) shows me how he or she feels about some issue, it helps me make up my own mind about the issue.	0.476
8.	I see my favorite TV star (person) as a real, down-to-earth person.	0.452
4.	I feel sorry for my favorite TV star (person) when he or she makes a mistake.	0.443
1.	I get a true understanding of my favorite TV star (person) when I see them on TV	0.380
2.	When my favorite TV star (person) jokes around with other people it makes the program easier to watch.	0.393
14.	I sometimes make remarks to my favorite TV star (person) when he or she makes a mistake.	0.264

Attachment interaction

We follow the approach adopted by Feeney and Noller (1992) and validate a three factor model for our Attachment Scale, using SPSS. Conceptually, the items that loaded on *Anxious-ambivalent* revolved around intimacy, love and dependence. The items that loaded on *Secure* invoked display and comfort in trusting and getting close to others. While items related to discomfort, dependency and abandonment loaded on the third factor of *Avoidant*. The factor loadings were in line with the findings in the Cole and Leets (1999) study as shown in Table 2.

Table 2. Attachment Styles Factor Loadings Attachment style scale items (Feeney & Noller, 1992)

Items		Factor 1 Anxious Ambivalent	Factor 2 Secure	Factor 3 Avoidant
2	Sometimes people are scared away by my wanting to be too close to them.	**0.552**	-0.171	-0.020
3	My partner often wants me to be more intimate than I feel comfortable being.	**0.585**	-0.160	0.115
13	I often worry that my partner doesn't really love me.	**0.663**	-0.207	-0.217
14	I want to merge completely with another person.	**0.635**	0.127	-0.140
5	I find that others are reluctant to get as close as I would.	**0.647**	-0.159	-0.096
6	I often worry that my partner won't want to stay with me.	**0.725**	-0.250	-0.079
4	I am nervous when anyone gets too close.	0.469	**-0.525**	0.006
8	I am somewhat uncomfortable being close to others.	0.465	**-0.493**	0.048
9	I find it relatively easy to get close to others.	0.406	**0.589**	0.198
10	I find it easy to trust others	0.471	**0.473**	-0.324
11	I feel comfortable depending on other people.	0.414	**0.470**	-0.444
12	I don't often worry about someone getting too close to me.	0.352	**0.565**	0.063
15	I often don't worry about being abandoned.	0.210	0.339	**0.503**
1	I find it difficult to depend on others.	0.295	-0.225	**0.624**
7.	I feel comfortable having other people depend on me.	0.442	0.325	**0.488**
	Extraction Method: Principal Component Analysis.			

4. Results And Discussion

The results were in line with our expectations where those who had secure attachment were found to be involved in weaker parasocial relationships (R

= 0.147). The correlation between PSR and avoidant was 0.373. While the correlation between PSR and Anxious-Ambivalent was much higher at 0.406. The test for differences in correlations coefficients indicates that the correlations are indeed significantly different at alpha of 0.05. We used factor analysis to assess the reliability and explore the dimensionality of the 21-item parasocial scale. The results summarized in Table 1 show that all items load well on a single factor and capturing 43.7% of the total variance, hence there was no need to eliminate any of items.

We use Pearson Correlation to determine the degree and nature of association between PSRs and the three attachment styles in our sample (Table1). We note that all correlation coefficients were statically significant at alpha of 0.05. More specifically, we theorized that the number of reported anxious-ambivalents and avoidants would be higher in the Kuwaiti sample than that in the North American studies found in the literature review and that the degree of parasocial relationships would be higher for anxious-ambivalents and avoidants in Kuwait than reported in the North American sample employed by Cole & Leets (1999). Through our study, we sought to expand the understanding of the relationships between parasocial relations and attachments in collectivist societies by focusing on Kuwait.

Overall, our results show thatKuwaitis and Kuwaiti residents form strong parasocial relationships. In general, our results were stronger than those reported in previous studies conducted in North America (Bond & Calvert, 2014; Cohen, 2004; Cohen, 1997; Cole& Leets, 1999); Dibble et al., 2015; Eyal & Cohen, 2006; Hazan & Shaver, 1987; Rubin et al., 1985; Woodley & Movius 2012) indicating that Kuwaitis and those living in Kuwait maybe turning to relatively stable TV characters as a means of satisfying their unrealistic and often unmet relational needs. The issue of gender segregation may also play a role. Gender segregation at many places (universities, places of worship, etc.) keeps the interaction between the two sexes at a minimum. As a result, inherent needs of love and friendship are difficult to satisfy in an environment that considers dating against societal norms and traditions. Turning to television idols creates a strong bond of intimacy, which would be difficult to feel in a traditional culture like Kuwait.

Furthermore, and as is the case for the Cole and Leets (1999) study, it was found that a person's willingness to form a parasocial bond with his or her favorite TV personality is related to his/her attachment type. There were statistical differences between the parasocial relationships of those who were secure, avoidant or anxious-ambivalent. It is possible that the parasocial bonds these individuals form with media figures simply reflects another manifestation of their desire for intimacy and the fulfillment of missing needs. In particular, we found a higher percentage of avoidants and anxious-ambivalents in our sample, and in return higher levels of insecure type parasocial relationships, with the latter group exhibiting the highest level of parasocial types of ties.

The percentage of those involved in insecure type relationships was 42.6% in the Cole and Leets (1999) study, that percentage in our study was 47.6%. The difference between the two was nearing significance and is in the direction expected, whereby the insecure-type attachment will be more prevalent in the collectivist setting as stipulated in Hypothesis 1.

What was also significant in this study is that those who classified as avoidants also seemed to have significant parasocial relationships in keeping with our hypotheses. This is counter to the findings of the Cole and Leets' (1999) study. It could be that being in a collectivist society where belonging to a group and forming strong ties are the norm, avoidants may have a higher tendency to seek "refuge" in a mediated bond.

Another difference between our results and those of Cole and Leets (1999) is that we found stronger correlations amongst the three types of attachment and PSRs. In this study, the highest correlation is for anxious-ambivalent, the second highest is for avoidants and the smallest is the secure type attachment. These results reinforce our hypotheses where we theorized that a high amount of avoidants and anxious-ambivalents would be found in our sample and that these two groups would both form the strongest parasocial bonds (See Table 3.).

Table 3. Correlation between Attachment Styles and Parasocial Relationship

	Cole & Leets' Study: Percentage respondents in each category & Correlation strength ranks N=159	Our Study: Percentage respondents in each category N=263	Our study: Correlations with PSRs & p-values N=263
1. PSR			1.0
2. Secure	57.4% (2)	52.5%	0.147* p = 0.07
3. Avoidant	24.3% (3)	27.3%	0.373** p = 0.00
4. Anxious	18.3% (1)	20.2%	0.406** p = 0.00

As Table 3 shows, the numbers of those belonging to the anxious-ambivalent and avoidant categories are higher than those reported in the Cole and Leets (1999) study. Hypothesis 2 is also supported as the correlations of PSR in the anxious-ambivalent and avoidant groups in Kuwait are higher than those reported in the Cole and Leets (1999) study.

Hypothesis 2 speaks to the degree of parasocial relationships and argues that this will be higher for anxious-ambivalent and avoidants. This is also supported as shown in Table 3. Another fascinating finding in the Kuwaiti sample was that the absolute majority of respondents (92 percent) reported having formed PSRs. It is plausible that maintaining such relationships is an expression of an inner-self that is kept hidden and is not allowed to be revealed in the society. In a conservative collectivist society, parasocial relationships may offer an outlet to engage in ties that may be more in line with one's inner or authentic self. Consequently, TV personalities may provide outlets for escape for viewers in the same way romance novels provide a fantasy world for women who are committed to reading them (Radway, 1991).

Our study has a number of limitations that should be outlined: First, our sample is limited to undergraduate students and as such is biased towards younger respondents. Cross-cultural researchers have identified age as an important variable that affects one's tendency to internalize the norms and values of the society and behave in a way that is in line with societal expectations (Triandis, 1995). Nonetheless, the Cole and Leets (1999) study also used university students as respondents.

The majority of the students in the Kuwaiti sample belong to affluent families, with multiple, nannies, drivers, and maids in each household. As described in the theory section, maids tend to assume many of the roles traditionally assigned to the mother. This phenomenon could be explored in future studies.

A related limitation is that the more affluent families tend to have access to a wide variety of media and foreign programming. As the children grow-up in a westernized environment where English may be widely spoken at home, they would be more likely to follow Western shows and programs.

References

Aboud, F. E., & Doyle. A. (1993). The early development of ethnic identity and attitudes. In M. E. Bernal & G. P. Knight (Eds.), *Ethnic identity: Formation and transmission among Hispanics and other minorities* (pp. 47-59). Albany, NY: State University of New York Press.

Adam, A. & Sizemore, B. (2013). Parasocial romance: A social exchange perspective. *Interpersona, 7(1)*, 12–25. doi:10.5964/ijpr.v7i1.106

Ainsworth, M. D. S., Blehar, M. S., Waters, E., & Wall, S. (1978). *Patterns of attachment: A psychological study of the strange situation*. Hillsdale, NJ: Erlbaum Publishers.

Al-Enezi, A. K. (2002). Kuwait's employment policy: Its formulation, implications, and challenges. *International Journal of Public Administration, 25(7)*, 885-900. doi:10.1081/pad-120004109

Al-Fuzai, M. (2014, Sept 25). Ana Kuwaiti! *Kuwait Times*.

Al-Jassar, M. A. (2009). *Constancy and Change in Contemporary Kuwait City: The Socio-cultural Dimensions of the Kuwait Courtyard and Diwaniyya* (Doctoral dissertation). Availablen from ProQuest Dissertations and Theses database. (UMI No. 3363409)

Auter, P. J. (1992). Psychometric: TV that talks back: An experimental validation of a parasocial interaction scale. *Journal of Broadcasting and Electronic Media, 36* (2),173–181. doi:10.1080/08838159209364165

Baldwin, J,R., Perry, S. D. & Moffitt, M. (2004). *Communication theories in everyday life*. Boston, MA: Allyn and Bacon/Pearson

Barakat, H. (1993). Arab identity: e pluribus unum. *The Arab world: Society, culture, and state*. Oakland, CA: The University of California Press.

Bernal, M., & Knight, G. (Eds). (1993*). Formation and transmission among Hispanics and other minorities.* New York: State University of New York Press.

Berns, R. (2013). *Child, family, school, community: Socialization and support.* Belmont, CA: Wadsworth/ Thomson Learning.

Blau, P. M. (1964). *Exchange and power in social life.* New York, NY: Wiley.

Bond, B.J., & Calvert, S.L. (2014). A model and measure of US parents' perceptions of young children's parasocial relationships. *Journal of Children & Media, 8(3),* 286 –304. doi:10.1080/17482798.2014.890948

Bowlby, J. (1969). *Attachment and loss: Vol. 1. Attachment.* New York: Basic Books.

Bowlby, J. (1973). *Attachment and loss: Vol. 2. Separation: Anxiety and anger.* New York: Basic Books.

Bowlby, J. (1980). *Attachment and loss: Vol. 3. Loss: Sadness and depression.* New York: Basic Books.

Bryant, J., & Oliver, M.B. (2009). *Media effects: Advances in theory and research (3rd ed.)..* New York, NY: Routledge.

Burnett, A., & Beto, R. R. (2000). Reading romance novels: An application of parasocial relationship theory. **The** *North Dakota Journal of Speech & Theatre,* **13,** 28-39.

Camella, C. (2001). Parasocial relationships in female college student soap opera viewers today. Retrieved June 2, 2008, from: http://people.wcsu.edu/mcarneyh/acad/camella.html

Cohen, J. (1997). Parasocial relations and romantic attraction: Gender and dating status differences. *Journal of Broadcasting & Electronic Media, 41*(4), 516-529. Retrieved from: http://www.jstor.org/

Cohen, J. (2003). Parasocial breakups: Measuring individual differences in responses to the dissolution of parasocial relationships. *Mass Communication & Society, 6 (2),* 191-202. doi:10.1207/s15327825mcs0602_5

Cohen, J, (2004). Parasocial break-up from favorite television characters: The role of attachment styles and relationships intensity. *Journal of Social and Personal Relationships, 21*(2), 187-202 Retrieved ,from: http://search.ebscohost.com

Cole, T., & Leets, L. (1999) Attachment styles and intimate television viewing: Insecurely forming relationships in a parasocial way. *Journal of Social and Personal Relationships, 16*(4), 495-511. doi:10.1177/0265407599164005

Cropanzano, R. & Mitchell, M. (2005). Social exchange theory: An interdisciplinary review. *Journal of Management, 31(6),*874-900. doi:10.1177/0149206305279602

Dakhli, M., Khorram, S., & Vora, D. (2007). Information management in multicultural groups: The role of network structure. Paper presented at Southern Management Association 2007 Meeting, Nashville, Tennessee, USA. Retrieved from https://southernmanagement.org/meetings/2007/proceedings/flashpop.htm

Dinkha, J., Abdulhamid, S., & Abdelhalim, N.. (2008). How identity is constructed in Kuwait: Analysis of four case studies. *Psychology Journal 5(4),* 190-211.

Dinkha, J., & Dakhli, M. (2009). Perceived discrimination in the Arabian Gulf: The case of migrant labor in Kuwait. *Psychology Journal, 6*(2), 47-59.

Earley, C. P. (1994). Self or groups? Cultural effects of training on self-efficacy and performance. *Administrative Science Quarterly 39*(1), 89-117. doi:10.2307/2393495

Erez, E., & Earley, C. (1993). *Culture, self identity and work.* Oxford University Press: New York.

Eyal, K., & Cohen, J. (2006). When good friends say goodbye: A parasocial breakup study. *Journal of Broadcasting & Electronic Media, 50*(3), 502-523. Retrieved from http://www.jstor.org/

Eyal, K. & Rubin, A. M. (2003). Viewer aggression and homophily, identification, and parasocial relationships with television characters. *Journal of Broadcasting & Electronic Media, 47*(1), 77-98.

Feeney, J. A., & Noller, P. (1990). Attachment style as a predictor of adult romantic relationships. *Journal of Personality and Social Psychology, 58,* 281–291.

Feeney, J. A., & Noller, P. (1992). Attachment style and romantic love: Relationship dissolution. *Australian Journal of Psychology, 44*(2), 69–74. doi:10.1080/00049539208260145

Feeney, J. A., Noller, P., & Patty, J. (1993). Adolescents' interactions with the opposite sex: Influence of attachment style and gender. *Journal of Adolescence, 16,* 169–186.

Gay, G. (1978). Multicultural preparation and teacher effectiveness in desegregated schools. *Taylor & Francis Group, 17(2),* 149-156. doi:10.1080/00405847809542758

Dibble, J. L., Hartmann, T., & Rosaen, S. F. (2015). Parasocial interaction and parasocial relationship: Conceptual clarification and a critical assessment of measures. *Human Communication Research.* doi:10.1111/hcre.12063

DiPiazza, F.D. (2007). *Kuwait in Pictures.* Minneapolis, MN: Lerner Publishing Company.

Hazan, C., & Shaver, P. (1987). Romantic love conceptualized as an attachment process. *Journal of Personality and Social Psychology, 52(3)*, 511-524.

Hofstede. G. (2001). *Culture's Consequences: Comparing Values, Behaviors, Institutions and Organizations Across Nations* (. 2nd ed.)- Thousand Oaks CA: Sage Publications.

Hofstede, G. (1980). *Culture's consequences: International differences in work-related values*. Beverly Hills, CA: Sage.

Hofstede, G. (1991). *Cultures and organizations: Software of the mind*. London: McGraw-Hill.

Horton, D., & Wohl, R. (1956). Mass communication and para-social interaction: Observations of intimacy at a distance.*Psychiatry, 19*(3), 215-229. Retrieved from: http://visual-memory.co.uk/daniel/Documents/short/horton_and_wohl_1956.html

James, R., & Gilliland, B. (2013). *Crisis intervention strategies* (7th ed). Belmont, CA: Cengage Learning.

Kagitcibasi, C. (1994). A critical appraisal of individualism and collectivism: Toward a new formulation., In U. Kim, H.C. Triandis, C. Kagitcibasi, S. Choi, and G. Yoon (Eds.), *Individualism and collectivism: Theory, method, and application* (pp. 52-65). Thousand Oaks, CA: Sage Publications.

Konishi, C., & Hymel, S. (2014). An attachment perspective on anger among adolescents. *Merrill-Palmer Quarterly, 60(1)*, 53–79.

Kluckhohn, F., & Strodbeck, F. (1961). *Variations in value orientation*. Evanston, Illinois: Harper & Row. .

Kuwait approves women's political rights *(2005, May 16)*. *USA Today*. Retrieved from http://www.usatoday.com/news/world/2005-05-16-kuwait-women_x.htm

Leighton, L. (1982). Lermontov: A study in literary-historical evaluation. *The American Association for the Advancement of Slavic Studies, 41(2),* 380-381. doi:10.2307/2496401

Lewis, F. (2000). Getting by: race and parasocial interaction in a television situation comedy. Retrieved May 19, 2008, from: http://dissertation.com/

Loew, H. *Culture of Kuwait* (n.d). Retrieved December 2, 2007, from: http://www.everyculture.com/Ja-Ma/Kuwait.html

Manusov V., & Harvey J. H. (2001). *Attribution, communication behavior, and close relationships.* Cambridge, UK: Cambridge University Press.

Marková, I., & Gillespie, A. (2008). *Trust and distrust: sociocultural perspectives.* USA: Information Age Publishing. -

Nathanson, A. I., & Manohar, U. (2012*).* Attachment, working models of parenting, and expectations for using television in childrearing. *Interdisciplinary Journal of Family Studies: Family Relations, 61*(3), 441 – 454. doi: 10.1111/j.1741-3729.2012.00701.x

Parsons, T. & Shils, E. A. (1951). *Toward a general theory of action.* Cambridge, MA: Harvard University Press.

Petrakis, E. (2014). *Culture, growth and economic policy.* New York, NY: Springer Publishers.

Phinney, J. S. (1990). Ethnic identity in adolescents and adults: A review of research. *Psychological Bulletin, 108* (3), 499-514. doi:10.1037//0033-2909.108.3.499

Phinney, J. S. (1991). Ethnic identity and self-esteem: A review and integration. *Hispanic Journal of Behavioral Sciences, 13 (2),* 193-208.

Pyke, K., & Bengtson, V. (1996). Caring more or less: Individualistic and collectivist systems of family eldercare. *Journal of Marriage and the Family, 58(2)*, 379-392. doi: 10.2307/353503

Radway, J. A. (1991). *Reading the romance: Women, patriarchy, and popular literature.* Chapel Hill, NC: University of North Carolina Press.

Rosenberg, M. (1979). *Conceiving the self.* New York: Basic Books.

Rizzo, H. M. (2005). *Islam, democracy, and the status of women: the case of Kuwait.* NY: Rutledge.

Rubin, A., Perse, E., & Powell, R. (1985). Development of parasocial interaction relationships. *Human Communication Research, 12, (2)*, 155-180.

Schiappa, E., Gregg, P., & Hewes, D. (2005). The parasocial contact hypothesis. *Communication Monographs, 72*, (1), 92-115. Retrieved June 2, 2008, from: http://www.jstor.org/

Schmitt, D. P., Alcalay, L., Allensworth, M., Allik, J., Ault, L., Austers, I., ... ZupanÈiÈ, A. , (2004) Patterns and universals of adult romantic attachment across 62 cultural regions. *Journal of Cross-Cultural Psychology, 35(4)*, 367-402. doi:10.1177/0022022104266105

Shah N.M., Al-Qudsi S., & Shah, M. (1991). Asian women workers in Kuwait. *International Migration Review, 25*(3), 464-486. doi:10.2307/2546756

Slade, A.F., Narro, A.J., & Buchanan, B.P. (2014). *Reality Television: Oddities of culture.* Lanham, Maryland: Lexington Books.

Sukrithan. S. (2009) Kuwait Times. Retrieved from: http://news.kuwaittimes.net/website

Tetreault, M., & Al-Mughni H. (1995). Gender, citizenship and nationalism in Kuwait. *British Journal of Middle Eastern Studies, 22*(1), 64-80. doi:10.1080/13530199508705612

Triandis, H. C. (1995). *Individualism and collectivism*. Boulder, CO:Westview. .

Triandis, H. C. (2001). Individualism-collectivism and personality. *Journal of Personality, 69(6)*, 907–924. doi:10.1111/1467-6494.696169

Wikhamn, W., & Hall, A. T. (2012). Social exchange in a Swedish work environment. *International Journal of Business and Social Science*, 3(23), 56-64.

Woodley, P., & Movius, L. (2012). PSI study results. University of Southern California.

Yamagishi, T. (2011). *Trust: The evolutionary game of mind and society*. New York, NY: Springer Publishers. .

You, H,S., & Malley- Morrison, K. (2000). Young adults attachment atyles and intimate relationships with close friends: A cross cultural study of Koreans and Caucasian Americans. *Journal of Cross-Cultural Psychology, 31(4)*, 528-534. doi: 10.1177/0022022100031004006

ACKNOWLEDGMENT: Special thank you to research assistant, Aya Abdulhamid (abdulhadi.aya@gmail.com) for her dedication and hard work in helping us to complete this chapter.

The Online Looking Glass: The Study of Self Esteem and Narcissism on Instagram Within a Patriarchal and Collectivist Society

By Juliet Dinkha, Charles Mitchell, Bashar Zogheib & Aya Abdulhadi

Abstract

Online social networking sites have revealed an entirely new method of impression management and self-expression. These user-generated social tools present a new and evolving medium of investigation to study personality and identity. The current study examines how narcissism and self-esteem are demonstrated on the social networking application Instagram. To frame our research, we utilized the Uses and Gratifications Theory, which explains why audiences consume mediated messages and how and why authors create user-generated media (UGM). In this research our objective was to understand how and why users of Instagram in Kuwait were using the social media platform and how it related and impacted their self-esteem and how it revealed, if any, narcissistic personality traits. To do so, self-esteem and narcissistic personality self-reports were collected from 79 Instagram users in Kuwait and we also followed and analyzed their Instagram accounts. In our analysis, these participants' profiles were coded on self-promotional content features based on their Instagram photos and captions posted on their Instagram accounts. By probing the relationship between this new medium, we can begin to understand the relationship amongst technology, culture, and the self.

Key words: social media, Kuwait, Instagram, self-esteem, narcissism, social networking

Introduction

The influence of mass media on its audience has been the subject of long-standing debate since the introduction of radio and TV as entertainment and information media in the early 20th century (Dominick, 2009). Since this time, media scholars have been looking for ways to study media and to ascertain what detrimental effects they have on their audience including but not limited to the cultivation effect, introducing a young audience to sexual and violent images, presenting unrealistic body images, creating aggressive modelling behaviors and desensitization to violence that can come from mass media consumption of TV, film and even video games (Murray, 2008; Perse & Lambert, 2008; Dominick, 2009). TV has been at the forefront of these studies as statistics indicate that children will spend more time in front of the TV than they will sleep by the time they are 18. Furthermore, by the time children are 18, they will have consumed more than 200,000 acts of television violence (Dominick, 2009). Along this line, it is often the significance of the influence of mass media on youth that has been the most widely studied and debated. Moreover, early scholars often focused on TV's violent effects with often polarizing conclusions. Most notably, in 1961, Albert Bandura published his seminal work on children's modelling behaviors after they watched adults engaging in violent activities on a video monitor (Black, 1995; Seawell, 1998; Murray, 2008; Dominick, 2009; Fisher et al., 2009; Dinkha, Mitchell, & Zogheib, 2014). The finding of this study indicated that people learn through imitation, modeling, and observing. Additionally, according to Bandura, people can learn through reward and punishment (Bandura, Ross, & Ross, 1961).

Since the rise of the Internet age in early 1990s, scholars have been carrying out research on how the Internet influences its audience given the propensity for television to affect its viewers. During the last several decades, the studies into Internet consumption have centered on political participation, democratic mobilization and the most recently the concept of cyber bullying. For the fields of psychology and mass communications, there remains a gap in the research realm for the study of self-esteem, self-perception; and how these variables relate to the concept of narcissism within user-generated media, specifically social media. In our study, we decided to fill this need and investigate the relationships amongst narcissism, self-esteem and social media because, social media users have been increasingly engaging in excessive and sometimes addictive use of social networking platforms (O'Keeffe & Clarke-Pearson 2011). We opted to focus on the Middle East due to the limited research on this topic in the region and given that the cultural nuances could provide opportunities for additional inquires. Furthermore, we are researchers from Western and Eastern backgrounds who live in Kuwait. Another reason we decided on this topic is because Arabian Gulf countries have some of the highest concentrations of social media consumption in the world; and there remains a gap in the research on this region on the subject matter (Maarefi, 2013). Furthermore, the Middle East is comprised of collectivist and patriarchal societies and would allow us the chance to discover if the authentic self is expressed in social networking given the need for individuals in the Arab world to often save face and uphold cultural mores and norms even during times of online engagement (Maarefi, 2013). As a country with one of the largest penetrations of social media usage among youth and young adults in the Middle East and the world (Maarefi, 2013), Kuwait provides the optimal platform for an interdisciplinary study encompassing mass communications and psychology on the relationships among social media, self-esteem and narcissism.

Moreover, Kuwait being a patriarchal society with different social mores for both men and women would provide additional research opportunities to ascertain if this variable has an affect on how males and females consume and utilize social media, including females being their authentic selves online versus adhering to gender roles proscribed by societal norms (Tétreault and Haya al-Mughn, 1995; Tétreault, 2001; Dinkha et al., 2008; Olimat, 2009).

Uses And Gratification Theory

The Uses and Gratification Theory (UGT) is the principal paradigm exploited to frame our research. We decided up on this theory as it provides the most robust and relevant model to our key reasons for inquiry which are to understand how and why Instagram users in Kuwait are utilizing the platform and specifically what it says about their self-esteem and narcissism.

UGT was developed primarily for and is employed in the field of the mass communication theory and states audiences choose mediate messages to satisfy their needs. The theory serves scholars as a guide to assess and evaluate audience reasons for consuming and accessing media. Specifically, UGT provides us with the personal motivations as to why and how people use mass media (Rubin, 2002; Stafford, Stafford & Schkade 2004; Shao, 2008: Urista, Dong & Day, 2009).

Traditionally, UGT has been exploited to study audience behaviors with respect to consumption of radio, television and cable TV. In the digital age, however it has already been exploited as model to gauge audience usage of news media channels because it concedes, acceptance, uses, and creation of recent technologies and messages. In the era of new media, UGT has been purposeful for inquiry into understanding audiences and users' satisfaction with Internet based platforms: those noted for being highly interactive, flexible and constantly evolving. It further helps to understand and study motivations of (User Generated Media) UGM that is endemic in social media platforms (Stafford et al., 2004; Shao, 2008).

McQuail (1983) identified four categories for why people select media: information, personal identity, integration and social interaction and lastly, entertainment. Recently however, media scholars have placed UGT into two principal categories that exemplify why audiences typically use the Internet: information and entertainment. Entertainment tells us that people seek messages on the Internet as they do with other forms of media such as movies and TV, often seeking out messages that will lift their mood, scare them or provide sexual arousal.

Despite the tremendous benefits of entertainment seeking, information too is vital and is linked to the idea that an individual wants to exploit media to create awareness of themselves, others or the world. More typically and more simply put, UGT suggests that the utilization of media offers some form of gratification and helps us to decipher motivations behind consumption and creation of media, including related outcomes such as consequences or benefits (Shao, 2008; Sheldon & Bryant, 2016). Matsuba (2006) tell us there is a third category, interpersonal communication, which emphasizes the desires for individuals to utilize the Internet to fulfill relational needs.

Since the purpose of our research is understand what the UGM-framed social media platform Instagram tells us about self-esteem and narcissism, then UGT serves as the most applicable model to guide our research. For example, users routinely monitor their own followers' comments, likes and feedback as an indication of how well they are doing for the goal of receiving positive reinforcement (Gentile et al., 2012; Sheldon & Bryant, 2016). Additionally, research has indicated that a correlation also exists between narcissism and the amount of time spent editing selfies before posting on social media, which confirms desire to be perceived positively by followers. This illustrates that users are seeking out online engagement as a compensatory need to be recognized and to satisfy the need for interpersonal communication (Dominick, 1999; Matsuba, 2006; Urista et al., 2009; Sheldon & Bryant, 2016). Before we progressed with our study; however, it was important for us to explore and to understand the two psychological terms and conditions which we are studying on Instagram: narcissism and self-esteem.

Narcissism

Psychologists describe narcissism as the egotistical preoccupation with the self, personal preferences, aspirations, needs, success, and how one is perceived by others (Lopez, 2008). Austrian psychoanalyst Otto Rank linked narcissism it to self-admiration and vanity. Psychoanalyst, Heinz Kohut (1968), originated the term narcissistic personality disorder. He suggested that narcissism allows people to suppress feelings of low self-esteem and develop their sense of self. In 1980, narcissistic personality disorder was recognized by the American Psychiatric Association's (APA) third edition of the Diagnostic and Statistical Manual of Mental Disorders (DSM-III) (Burgemeester, 2013).

There is now a comprehensive body of scientific research that focuses on narcissism and it has become a more widely understand phenomenon. According to (Mayo Clinic, 2014) narcissistic personality disorder is characterized by dramatic and emotional behavior and a polarizing range of symptoms: The disorder's symptoms may include believing that you are better than others and that you are special, being easily hurt and rejected, seeking constant praise and admiration, and having a fragile self-esteem. A narcissist has trouble handling criticism, and to make themselves feel better, they react with rage and will do their best to belittle others so they would appear to be in the right.

The behavior characterized as narcissistic injury posits that a narcissist is sensitive to criticism and perceives those who disagree with their point of view as a threat and may take criticism itself as some type of form of rejection. They also tend to detach emotionally in fear of another narcissistic injury, and they devalue the person from whom they received the negative critique (Deconstructingjezebel, 2015).

It is argued that narcissistic individuals use social media because they offer a highly controllable environment where users can exhibit complete control over the way they present themselves. Another reason narcissists are attracted to social media sites is due to the capacity to maintain shallow relationships as they would ordinarily prefer over deeper interpersonal ones (Sheldon & Bryant, 2016, p.89). In contrast to all other social media platforms, the nature of Instagram shifts the focus of individuals toward the self, thus, self-promotion and an identity focus are prioritized over actual face-to-face relationships. On Instagram, posting selfies is commonplace and is an expression of individuality. In comparison to other social media sites, Instagram is relatively more intimate, in which people share personal images such as pictures taken in their homes; whereas with Twitter for example, the user is constrained by a Tweet with limited characters and pictures are not necessary (Bradford, 2018).

Self-Esteem

As mentioned previously, the UGT would surmise that some of the reasons why individuals consume mediated messages such as social media is it because it reinforces behaviors and responses that can build positive self-esteem, including bolstering personal value and self-understanding (Gentile et al., 2012; Sheldon & Bryant, 2016). Historically, self-esteem refers to a person's positive or negative evaluation of the self; that is, the extent to which an individual views the self as worthwhile and competent (Coopersmith, 1967). According to one definition by Braden in 1969, there are three key components of self-esteem: Firstly, self-esteem is an essential human need that is vital for survival and normal healthy development. Secondly, self-esteem arises automatically from within, based upon a person's principles and consciousness. Thirdly, self-esteem occurs in conjunction with a person's thoughts, behaviors, feelings and actions. Self-esteem is expressed differently from one person to another, since it is developed through subjective experiences and interpersonal relationships. For instance, failing to meet parental standards during childhood can contribute to lowering the person's self-esteem in the future (Coopersmith, 1967).

Those who display low self-esteem view themselves pessimistically. If they experience failure of some sort for instance, in the form of romantic rejections, unsuccessful job experiences, or any form of criticism, they take it personally and feel as if the unfortunate string of events is confirming their opinion of their worth. Experts call this occurrence negative validation. A 2014 study published in the *Journal of Personality and Social Psychology* by researchers from the University of Waterloo and Wilfrid Laurier University, found people with low self-esteem generally don't prefer optimism and would rather believe the negative comments they think about themselves are true (Olson, 2014).

Martha Beck is an American sociologist, life coach, best-selling author, and speaker who specializes in helping individuals and groups achieve personal and professional goals. In 2014, she published an article titled *How to Handle the Narcissists in Your Life* for O magazine. Under the section 'How to Tell Healthy Self-Esteem from Narcissism' the author explains that people with a healthy self-esteem seek ways to improve themselves and would invent a long list of attributes they want to improve if confronted with the question: In what ways do you think you need to grow or change? On the other hand, narcissists will claim that they have nothing to change because admitting that they are imperfect is a difficult idea for them to process or express (Beck, 2014).

Virtual Communities & Social Networking Sites

Virtual communities such as social networking sites like YouTube, LinkedIn, Facebook and Instagram are used as social platforms to establish and sustain friendships, and communicate with friends, colleagues and relatives at long or short distances, which provide users a way to feel connected to other people and as valuable means of self-expression. It has been theorized that people use virtual communities or social networking sites (SNS) because they desire to experience an instant and personal connection to others and as means of seeking approval and support (Urista et al., 2009).

For instance, the popularity of social media platforms such as Facebook and YouTube can be correlated to the social interaction and self-gratification these virtual communities provide to the users as public conversations online can deliver a sense of intimacy and often build and sustain and personal relationships. The advantages of these online communities are that they allow like-minded people to find each other and to form ties based on similarities and common interests (Shao, 2008; Urista et al., 2009). Likewise, it has been observed that people often engage in virtual communities because it provides them with a sense of fitting in and belonging (Shao, 2008). Along this line, a new generation of social media savvy Internet denizens have emerged whose identities are based on content generation and their social media friends, connections and followers (Urista et al., 2009).

Davenport, S. et al., 2014 asserts that two types of social networking expressions exist: active usage and passive usage. Active usage is displayed through engaging and creation of content on social media sites or website such as blogs, while passive usage is displayed through browsing and listening to content created by other users. On social media these two dynamics are typically on display where authors (active and frequent users) often create and share content with other followers (passive users) by posting likes, adding comments, saving favorites or sharing on their own accounts (Chan, 2006). However, researchers observe that often causal browsers themselves became more active as they move from mere observer to participant by engaging in posting, sharing and liking, which are behaviors typical of active users (Shao, 2008).

Given the flexible and customizable nature of social media Shao (2008) identifies UGM as being instrumental to these virtual communities because it enables users an important mode of self-expression. Self-expression on social media communities is offered in the form of videos, blogging, photos and other posts. The UGM allow authors to express and present their authentic selves or to share a side of themselves they see inside. These communities and platforms help the individual to project and craft an image of themselves to a larger audience than those in their immediate physical world (Dominick, 1999, Smith, 1999, Trammell and Keshelashvili, 2005; Shao, 2008).

Kuwait, The Internet And Social Media

The contribution of the Internet in Kuwait has been revolutionary in that it has been proven to be an essential platform for liberation, personal sovereignty, the ideas of democracy and democratic reforms (Kaposi, 2014). The Internet as a tool of social exchange has led to an explosion in blogging activity and as one respondent in Wheeler (2003) surmised at the time, it might have helped women to secure the right to vote.

Today, the Internet, and especially social media, has become the most important media vehicle for socializing with friends and family, keeping up with celebrity fandom, trend watching, gossiping and exchanging modes of thought (Kaposi, 2014; Wheeler, 2003). Both Wheeler and Kaposi observed that the Internet is used by the youth to bypass traditional societal norms of dating and gender segregation; as the youth readily use the Internet and social media to attract and to socialize with the potential dating partners. Furthermore, when surveyed many youth in Kuwait seemed to signify that Internet exchanges and posts allowed them to 'escape' and to be their authentic selves and they expressed a sense of self-liberation, which may be contrary to the roles they have to play in their everyday lives due to cultural mores (Kaposi 2014; Wheeler, 2000; Wheeler, 2003). "The more taboo a topic, the more likely it is to show up in chat rooms. The more Kuwaiti society tries to separate the genders, the more likely the Internet will be used to transgress such boundaries" (Wheeler, 2003, p. 14).

In Kuwait, the success of social media amongst the youth can be further attributed not only to the personal freedoms it provides but because it is perceived as hip and as an outlet to be fashionable and up-to-date on the newest fads (Kaposi, 2014).

In consequence, the virtual social world has led Kuwait to exceptional high rates of usage of social platforms, such as Twitter, Snapchat and Instagram. According to Maarefi (2013) Kuwait is the Arabian Gulf country with the highest social media use per capita. Although no clear data exists about the number of Instagram users from Kuwait, simply searching for pictures hash tagged with Kuwait would present you with 19.1 million pictures. Markedly, that is approximately 1 million less than pictures tagged with USA, a country with ten-fold Kuwait's population, on a search conducted on October 2014. Figure 1. illustrates the penetration of popular social media usage in Kuwait by age group:

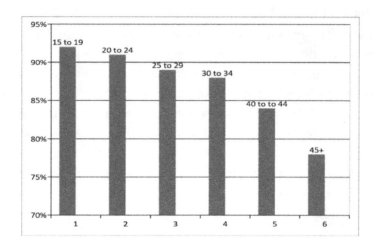

Figure 1. Social Media penetration in Kuwait by age group according to Ipsos MENA.

In Kuwait, with the popularity of Instagram came a new phenomenon of Instagram celebrities. An example of this is @Ascia. Ascia is popular Kuwaiti-based fashion blogger. With the explosion of Instagram in the country she now has 2.2 million followers when perused on July 2017, and charges upwards of 850 KD ($ 2,550) for one Instagram post Ascia's following is indicative of the high Instagram penetration in Kuwait when factoring in the country has a population of 3.9 million people (CIA World Factbook, 2014), and even when considering that many of her followers may well reside outside of the country.

Hypotheses:

1. The need to fulfill their relational and social needs in a collective society of Kuwait will lead to majority of our sample to qualify as frequent users of Instagram.
2. The activity level of users of Instagram in Kuwait will report narcissistic personality traits and high self-esteem.
3. Due to the patriarchal nature of Kuwait, male narcissistic respondents will outnumber female narcissistic respondents.
4. Narcissistic respondents are expected to self-promote and reinforce positive qualities about themselves through captions, pictures such as selfies, and photos of possessions than those of non-narcissistic respondents.

Research Method

We utilized a convenient sample of 79 Instagram account owners within Kuwait out of a sample of 100 accounts, who were randomly recruited from Kuwait. The sample included both Kuwaiti and non-Kuwaitis. Their educational level ranged from high school to postgraduate levels. Their ages ranged from 18-25 years. Please see *Criteria* for further explanation.

Procedure.

Instagram users in Kuwait were identified and then approached through two different methods: (1) Some participants were identified and contacted through Instagram direct messaging and asked to participate in a study exploring their use of Instagram (2) Student researchers also approached students on campus of a private university in Kuwait and recruited students who had Instagram accounts and who expressed an interest in participating.

The research team created an account on Instagram to gain and gauge participants for the study. We posted four posts including information about the study and who could participate. The selection process was restricted to participants who are in the age group of 18-25, residing in Kuwait, and completed the online survey sent via e-mail. The first post was about the research project with a brief description that we were studying usage of Instagram in Kuwait and encouraged people who were interested in the study to contact us via e-mail if they had questions. The second and third posts were to inform participants to accept our 'follow' requests on Instagram after completing the survey. The fourth post was about what participants need to do to participate in the research. Lastly, some of our research team members used their personal Instagram accounts to inform people about the study.

Criteria

All of those who were interested in participating were identified and selected on the basis of whether they had an active Instagram account. Active users were placed into three categories: 1. High rate of postings (e.g. more than 3 a day, daily) 2. Moderate rate of postings, (e.g. every other day, weekly) 3. Low rate of postings (e.g. biweekly, monthly). We found that the rate of postings did not correlate to self-esteem or narcissism, so all categories were combined in our statistics.

Upon agreeing to participate in this research study, participants were presented with a waiver form to sign if they consented to being followed on Instagram to have their page rated. Participants were also assured that all identifying information would be kept anonymous. Following their consent, participants were administered a four-part questionnaire. Upon completion, participants were immediately followed on Instagram and the process of rating and coding their pages began. The participants were aged between 18 and 25 years; they resided in Kuwait and had agreed and signed the consent form. The participants also completed the online survey sent to them via e-mail. Please see tables 1, 2 and 3.

For the purpose of reliability and validity six raters (3 males and 3 females) who were in the same age category as our sample were used to evaluate five self-promoting features of participants' Instagram: (a) The biography section, (b) The profile picture (c) The content of the first 15 pictures, (d) The frequency of uploading pictures, (e) Captions under photos.

For the purpose of this study, self-promotion was distinguished as any descriptive or visual information that appeared to attempt to persuade others about one's own positive qualities. For example, facial expression (e.g., striking a pose or making a face) and picture enhancement (e.g., using photo editing software) were coded in the profile picture and uploaded pictures. The use of positive adjectives (e.g., nice, sexy, funny), self-promoting mottos (e.g., 'I'm so glamorous I bleed glitter'), and/or positively descriptive hashtags were also noted.

Users whose native content was edited and enhanced prior to being posted, and frequently post on their native page with carefully chosen captions and elevated tone of voice are more likely to possess the characteristics of narcissism and high self-esteem compared to users who do not spend time to edit their content or self-promote in any measure.

Questionnaire Construction.

After agreeing to participate in this research study, Instagram owners were administered a brief four-part questionnaire. The first section required demographic information, including the participant's age and gender. The second section addressed their Instagram activity; it required respondents to indicate the number of times they checked their Instagram page per day and the time spent on Instagram per session. The remaining sections assessed two psychological constructs: self-esteem and narcissism. Prior to administering it to the participants, this questionnaire was distributed to 40 people for trial and feedback purposes.

The Rosenberg Self-Esteem Scale was used to measure the participants' self-esteem. The original reliability of this scale is 0.72. This measure has gained acceptable internal consistency and test-retest reliability, as well as convergent and discriminant validity. The Narcissism Personality Inventory (NPI-16) was also used. It is a short, efficient, and a valid mean to measure narcissism. It is composed of 16 questions.

In order to develop our rating criteria, we utilized categories from *The Impression Management 2.0 The Relationship of Self-Esteem, Extraversion, Self-Efficacy,* and *Self-Presentation Within Social Networking Sites* by Nicole C. Krämer and Stephan Winter (2008). The rating of the images was based on the following categories as illustrated below (Figure 3). Additionally, a training session was conducted to train the coders for this project on how to apply the rating criteria and examine the profiles for the purpose of the study.

Measure	Variables
Biography	-Formal (Similar to CV) -Informal -No bio
Links to other social media sites	-Yes -No
Captions	-Self promoting text -Informal text -No captions
Profile Picture	-Real photo of the user -Picture of other (celebrity etc.) -No photo
Post Rates	-Frequent posts (Daily) -Moderate (Weekly) -Infrequently (monthly or more)
Face visibility	-Completely -Partly -Not visible
Type of posts	-Selfies -Portraits -Possessions -Text -Interests -Landscapes -Family, friends and pets
Facial expression/ pose	-Model style pose -Picture taken while doing an action (For example playing a sport) -Serious (CV style photo)
Photo Edits	-Edited -No Edits
Location	-Yes -No

Figure 2. Categories formulated to rate photos on participants' social media account, Instagram.

The difference is in our research versus Kramer and Winter (2008) is that we included *Types of posts* which include Selfies, portraits, possessions, text, interests, landscapes, family, friends and pets. These criteria were included due to the diverse types of photos Instagram users post on their accounts. In our research, we also included the post rate which is a measure of the frequency of posts. Captions under photos were also considered. For example, self-advocating hashtags, or self-promoting photo descriptions. In the biography section the raters also looked at whether the users included links to other social media accounts. The similarity between the two scales is that they both examined the criteria for photo edits, location, face visibility, style of profile text, and facial expression pose.

Results

This study was administrated online where 79 participants from Kuwait were involved. Table 1 shows the number of female and male participants were almost identical. The p value of 0.03 of the Chi-Square test (Table 3) showed that males are more narcissistic than females. The analysis found that no difference between genders in the number of bios they post. It was also found in our sample that no difference between people activities on Instagram and whether they are considered narcissistic or have low self-esteem.

Table 1
Gender Analysis of Participants

	Frequency	Percent	Valid Percent	Cumulative Percent
Female	39	49.4	49.4	49.4
Male	40	50.6	50.6	100.0
Total	79	100.0	100.0	

Table 2		Frequency	Percent	Valid Percent	Cumulative Percent
Valid	Kuwait	76	96.2	96.2	96.2
	other	2	2.5	2.5	98.7
	3.00	1	1.3	1.3	100.0
Valid	less than highschool	1	1.3	1.3	1.3
	some highschool	1	1.3	1.3	2.5
	highschool	26	32.9	23.9	35.4
	some college	40	50.6	50.6	86.1
	college	9	11.4	11.4	97.5
	postgraduate	2	2.5	2.5	100
	Total	79	100	100	

Educational level was not related to self-esteem nor narcissism.

Table 3
Chi-Square Tests

	Value	Df	Asymp. Sig. (2-sided)	Exact Sig. (2-sided)	Exact Sig. (1-sided)
Pearson Chi-Square	4.255[a]	1	.039		
Continuity Correction[b]	3.153	1	.076		
Likelihood Ratio	4.387	1	.036		
Fisher's Exact Test				.048	.037
Linear-by-Linear Association	4.201	1	.040		
N of Valid Cases	79				

It was found from the table below that the number of female participants who scored below 15 was 37 and that of male was 33. Only 9 participants scored more than 15. 15 or higher is considered as displaying high esteem.

Table 4
Analysis of Self-Esteem

		Self-Esteem		Total
		Below 15	15 or more	
Gender	Female	37	2	39
	Male	33	7	40
Total		70	9	79

Table below shows that the number of female participants who scored 7 or above on the narcissistic test was 8 and that of males who scored 9 or above was 12.

Table 5
Analysis of Narcissism

	Narcissism		Total
Female	Below 7 31	7 or more 8	39
Male	Below 9 28	9 or more 12	40

It was also found that there is no correlation between narcissism and self-esteem. For males 9 or more indicates narcissism and for females 7 or higher indicates narcissism.

Discussion

This research looked at the relationship between narcissism indicated in the Rosenberg self-esteem criteria (see appendix) and the Narcissism Personality Inventory (NPI-16) (see appendix) and narcissism expressed in the use of the social media web and application platform Instagram. Our results proposed no direct relationship between narcissism and self-esteem with gender on Instagram. However, the results show that respondents may score highly on the narcissism scale in the survey and low narcissism expression on

Instagram or low on the narcissism scale in the survey and high on narcissism expression on Instagram. Additionally, results are consistent with the literature on gender differences with men scoring higher on the narcissism scale than woman (see table 5).

The results of our research may seem on the surface to indicate that there are no correlations between narcissism, self-esteem and Instagram. However, there could be myriad reasons why our results proved that there was no correlation: For example, Kuwait is a collectivist society and thusly the sense of self is shaped through a socialization process that puts the emphasis not on the self but on the family unit (Kluckhohn & Strodbeck, 1961; Gay, 1978; Leighton, 1982; Al-Jassar, 2009; Hofstede, 1991; Berns, 2013). In a collectivist society like Kuwait, the individual is constantly evaluating themselves based on their relationship to the family unit and to the larger society's collective identity in an effort to conform to group norms and not to stand out as an individual (Phinney, 1991; Bernal & Knight, 1993; Berns, 2013).

As a matter of consequence, there is a strong propensity to confirm to the social mores and not to violate any of these norms even if they are not a true reflection of the authentic self. In Kuwait society, high standards of living and boasting of material wealth is one way in which narcissistic behavior would be apparent. Boasting would be a symptom of narcissism and pictures of material possessions were readily posted on the Instagram accounts across our sample. Nevertheless, narcissism was not widely identified when our sample was surveyed. So, in doing so, our sample may display narcissistic behaviors on Instagram but when surveyed they may fill in the NPI questionnaire with responses that are more aligned to societal norms. On the surface these responses would seem to preclude narcissism and would place emphasis on being humble, altruistic and selfless even if these qualifies are not emblematic of our respondents' authentic selves. Our hypotheses proposed that narcissists were expected to post self-promoting photos and post quotes and texts that are self-promoting or indicate high self-esteem; The users in the sample that we examined posted photos of their possessions often which is a sign of narcissistic behavior where prestige is attached to luxury possessions, which was found in Charoensukmongkol's (2016) study on narcissism.

In addition, our hypotheses suggested that narcissist respondents were expected to post more selfies, post more portraits, than non-narcissist respondents. Due to cultural factors such as modesty and cultural shame, certain individuals make their Instagram accounts private and then capitalize on this privacy to express their true self expressions to their close circle of friends, and who may be less judgmental and even supportive of their actions, and which may seem to cultural traditionalists as violating social norms. Congruently, these variables may explain the oddities found in our results.

The Western-centric nature of the NPI test, is also likely a causal factor that negated us finding the results as posited in our hypotheses. The questions on the NPI were composed in a manner in which those who are deemed narcissistic from a Western standpoint would self-identify through their answers. However, the socialization of Kuwait would impel many, if not most, to negate their narcissistic authentic selves and fill in questions that are more aligned with societal norms. For example, question one asks (a) "I would really like to be the center of attention" or (b) "It makes me uncomfortable to be the center of attention." In an individualistic society the standard respondent displaying narcissistic behaviors would check 'a'; however, in Kuwait being the center of attention would be considered a deviation from cultural norms and so the respondent is more likely to check 'b' as their answer even if they are a narcissist. Question 2 asks (a) "I am no better or worse than most people "or (b) "I think I am a special person". Once again, according to the social norms of Kuwait even the most narcissistic person would likely check 'b' as their answer even if it is not reflective of the authentic self.

Accordingly, there is a propensity to abide by the norms, customs and traditions of the Kuwaiti society, even if these are not consistent with the inner authentic self (Dinkha et al., 2008). While our results for self-esteem reported were higher than narcissism, only nine participants scored more than 15, which is considered as displaying high self-esteem, and the rest were considered be within the range of low self-esteem.

We posit that the same phenomenon being that a Western-centric questionnaire encumbered participant from being honest about their true self-worth. For example, statement 1 reads, "On a whole I am satisfied with myself". Respondents may be more apt to choose to disagree or slightly disagree because it is more in line with cultural attitudes towards being humble. Correspondingly, statement 6 reads, "I do not have much to be proud of". Again, the socialization in society towards modesty may impel those to report 'disagree' or 'strongly disagree' even if those answers are not consistent with the inner self.

Several informal studies in blogs such as Psychology Today in the west presume that a high rate of selfies and photo editing are associated with an inflated self-esteem. While it may be true in the west, our study proves otherwise in Kuwait (Myers, 2013). As we have postulated, our results could be correlated to the nature of the society itself.

Limitations

The number of participants

In the preliminary stage of this research paper, over a hundred surveys were disseminated. However, during the survey coding and Instagram rating processes, many of the participants were deemed invalid, due to not accurately completing the survey, or not accepting our 'follow request' during the process of Instagram accounts rating. There was also a challenge in dissemination of the survey because of Instagram doesn't allow links to be sent to other users with the questionnaires linking to a third-party site such as Survey Monkey or Google Docs.

Kuwait has very stringent defamation laws which covers online conversation and spreading of rumors. With recent bombing incident in the region, the government has toughened these measures and has warned both citizens and expatriates of the consequences of spreading rumors online (Duffy, n.d; Toumi, 2015). This climate leads to increased paranoia among social media users about what information they are sharing and with whom.

Many things might explain why the participants completed the survey but did not grant us access to their Instagram accounts. It could be that their accounts were inactive by the time we were ready to rate, or it could also be due to cultural reasons such as people not feeling comfortable with the idea of anonymous people perusing their personal pictures and posts. Regardless of the reasons, a viable way to counter this limitation in the future is to follow the participant's account concurrently with survey administering. This would be more efficient and would ensure access to the participants' Instagram accounts.

Incorporating a different population

When this research was at its infancy, it was attempted to also incorporate Saudi Arabia. However, since the researchers of this study are based in Kuwait, attempting to reach a large number of participants virtually was deemed to be a difficult task. Most of the successful surveys were administered in hard copies in the at a private university in Kuwait. Additionally, Saudi Arabia's population is even more conservative than Kuwait's, making it even harder to collect data when not residing directly in that country. In the future, when seeking to administer a survey in another country, utilizing a research partner who resides in that country would be a wise strategy.

References

Al-Jassar, M. K. A. (2009). *Constancy and Change in Contemporary Kuwait City: The Socio-cultural Dimensions of the Kuwait Courtyard and Diwaniyya*. ProQuest.

Al-Otaibi, O. (1990). The development of planned shopping centres in Kuwait. *Retailing environments in developing countries*, 96-117.

Alsuwailan, Z. F. (2006). *The impact of societal values on Kuwaiti women and the role of education* (unpublished doctoral dissertation). University of Tennessee-Knoxville, Knoxville, TN

Bandura, A., Ross, D., & Ross, S. A. (1961). Transmission of aggression through imitation of aggressive models. *The Journal of Abnormal and SocialPsychology, 63*(3), 575.

Barakat, H. (1993). Arab identity: e pluribus unum. *The Arab world: Society, culture, and state*. Oakland, CA: The University of California Press.

Beck, M. (2003, August). How to Handle the Narcissists in Your Life. Retrieved from http://www.oprah.com/omagazine/Martha-Beck-Self-Esteem-or-Narcissism http://www.oprah.com/omagazine/Martha-Beck-Self-Esteem-or-Narcissism

Bernal, M., & Knight, G. (Eds). (1993). *Formation and transmission among Hispanics and other minorities*. New York: State University of New York Press.

Berns, R. (2013). *Child, family, school, community: Socialization and support*. Belmont, CA: Wadsworth.

Black, D., Newman, M., (1995) Television Violence and Children: Its Effects Need To Be Seen In The Context of Other Influences on Children's Mental Health. BMJ: *British Medical Journal*, Vol. 310, No. 6975), pp. 273-274

Bradford, A., (February 4 2018) Everything you need to master Instagram Stories. Retrieved, April 2 2018, from https://www.cnet.com/how-to/how-to-use-instagram-stories/

Burgemeester, A. (2013, April 18). The History of Narcissistic Personality Disorder. Retrieved June 24, 2014, from http://thenarcissisticlife.com/the-history-of-narcissistic-personality-disorder/ http://thenarcissisticlife.com/the-history-of-narcissistic-personality-disorder/

Central Intelligence Agency. (2015, July 15). The World Factbook: Kuwait. Retrieved June 24, 2014, from: https://www.cia.gov/library/publications/the-world-factbook/geos/ku.html

Chan, A. (2006), "Social interaction design case study: MySpace", available at: http://www.gravity7.com/G7_SID_case_myspace_v2.pdf (accessed February 15, 2019).

Charoensukmongkol, P. (2016). Exploring personal characteristics associated with selfie-liking. *Cyberpsychology: Journal of Psychosocial Research on Cyberspace, 10*(2).

Cherry, K. (n.d.). What is self-esteem? Retrieved June 24, 2014, from http://psychology.about.com/od/sindex/f/what-is-self-esteem.htm

Coopersmith, S. (1967). *The Antecedents of Self Esteem.* San Francisco, CA. Freeman.

Dakhli, M., Dinkha, J., Matta, M., Aboul-Hosson, N. (2013). *The Effect of Culture and Gender on Coping Strategies: An Extension Study.* International Journal of Social Science. 8.(1), 87-98

Davenport, S., Bergman, S., Bergman, J., & Fearrington, M. (2014). Twitter versus Facebook: Exploring the role of narcissism in the motives and usage of different social media platforms. *Computers in Human Behavior,* 32, pp213. doi:10.1016/j.chb.2013.12.011

Deconstructingjezebel. (n.d.). What is Narcissism: narcissistic injury. Retrieved from http://www.deconstructingjezebel.com/narcissistic-injury.html

Dinkha, J., Abdulhamid, S., & Abdelhalim, Nur. (2008). How identity is constructed in Kuwait: Analysis of four case studies. *Psychology Journal 5(4)*, 190-211.

Dinkha, J., Mitchell, C., & Zogheib, B. (2014). Parental Control: the Relationship

Amongst Parental Supervision, Education, Income and Children's Viewing Habits.*American Journal of Humanities and Social Sciences*, 2(3), 157-170.

Dominick, J. (1999), "Who do you think you are? Personal home pages and self-presentation on the world wide web", Journalism and Mass Communication Quarterly, Vol. 76 No. 4, pp. 646-58.

Dominick, Joseph, R (2009). The Dynamics of Mass Communication: Media in the Digital Age. New York, NY: McGraw-Hill

Donn, G., & Al Manthri, Y. (Eds.). (2013). Education in the Broader Middle East: borrowing a baroque arsenal. Symposium Books Ltd.

Duffy, M. (n.d) Media laws and regulations of the GCC countries: Summary, analysis and recommendations.*Doha Centre for Media Freedom.* Retrieved on July 13, 2015 fromhttp://www.dc4mf.org/sites/default/files/gcc_media_law_en_0.pdf

Duggan, M., Ellison, N., Lampe, C., Lenhart, A., & Madden, M. (2015, January 9). Social Media Update 2014. *PewResearchCenter*. Retrieved April 1, 2015, from http://www.pewinternet.org/files/2015/01/PI_SocialMediaUpdate20144pdf

EEAS, European External Action. (2016). EU relations with the Gulf Cooperation Council (GCC.) Retrieved July 11, from http://eeas.europa.eu/gulf_cooperation/ index_en.htm

Fisher, A. F., Hill, D.L., Grube, J.W., Bersamin, M. M., Walker, S., Gruber, E.L. (2009) Televised sexual content and parental mediation: Influences on adolescent sexuality. *Media Psychol.* Jan 1, 2009; 12(2): 121–147.

Seawell M. (1998) *National Television Violence Study.* Vol 3. Thousand Oaks, CA: Sage. https://eric.ed.gov/?id=ED420437

Gay, G. (1978). Multicultural preparation and teacher effectiveness in desegregated schools. *Taylor & Francis Group, 17(2)*, 149-156.

Gentile, B., Twenge, J. M., Freeman, E. C., & Campbell, W. K. (2012). The effect of social networking websites on positive self-views: An experimental Investigation. *Computers in Human Behavior, 28*(5), 1929-1933.

Hofstede, G. (1991). *Culture and organizations: Software of the mind.* London: McGraw-Hill.

Howard, P., Duffy, A., Freelon, D., Hussain, M., Mari, W., &Mazaid, M. (2011). Opening Closed Regimes: What Was the Role of Social Media During the Arab Spring? *SSRN Electronic Journal.*Retrieved from http://pitpi.org/wp-content/uploads/2013/02/2011_Howard-Duffy-Freelon-Hussain-Mari-Mazaid_pITPIPDF

Ipos MENA. (2014). Social Media Users Who Access Social Media Daily,2012-2013[Graph]. Retrieved from http://www.slideshare.net/mobile/IpsosMENA/digitalmedia-forum-dhttp://www.slideshare.net/mobile/IpsosMENA/digitalmedia-forum-d

Jena, A. (2011, December 12). Different types of self esteem. Retrieved from http://www.projectguru.in/publications/types-of-self-esteem/

Kaposi, I. (2014). The culture and politics of Internet use among young people in Kuwait.*Cyberpsychology: Journal of Psychosocial Research on Cyberspace,8*(3), article 1. doi: 10.5817/CP2014-3-9

Kluckhohn, F., &Strodbeck, F. (1961). *Variations in value orientation.* Evanston, Illinois: Harper & Row.

Kohut, H. (1968). Narcissistic personality disorders: outline systematic approach., *Psychoanal. Study Child*, 23:86-113.

Krämer, N. C., &Winter, S. (2008). Impression management 2.0: The relationship of self-esteem, extraversion, self-efficacy, and self-presentation within social networking sites. *Journal of Media Psychology*, 20(3), 106-116.

Lau, A., Gabarron, E., Fernandez-Luque, L., &Armayones, M. (2012). Social media in health – what are the safety concerns for health consumers? *Health Information Management*, 41. Retrieved from http://www.himaa2.org.au/HIMJ/sites/default/files/HIMJ 41-2 Lau et al PDF

Leighton, L. (1982). Lermontov: A study in literary-historical evaluation. *The American Association for the Advancement of Slavic Studies, 41(2),* 380-381.

Li, K., & Lu, H. (2011). Why people use social networking sites: An empirical study integrating network externalities and motivation theory. *Computers in Human Behavior, 27*(13), 1152–1161.

Living in Saudi Arabia. (n.d.). Retrieved from http://www.internations.org/saudi-arabia-expats/guide/living-in-saudi-arabia-15364 http://www.internations.org/saudi-arabia-expats/guide/living-in-saudi-arabia-15364

Loew, H. *Culture of Kuwait.* Retrieved December 2, 2007, from: http://www.everyculture.com/Ja-Ma/Kuwait.html

Maarefi, S. (2014, July 17). KUNA: Social media gaining more leverage in Kuwait, needs optimization experts. Retrieved from http://www.kuna.net.kw/ArticleDetails.aspx?id=2322334&Language=en

Matsuba, K. (2006). Searching for self and relationships online. *CyberPsychology & Behavior*, 9(3), 275-284.

McQuail, D. (1983), "Mass Communication Theory", 1st ed., Sage, London.

Mayo Clinic. (2014). *Narcissistic personality disorder Symptoms*. Retrieved from http://www.mayoclinic.org/diseases-conditions/narcissistic-personality-disorder/basics/symptoms/con-20025568

Mitchell, C., Dinkha, A., Kononova, A., Rashwan, T., Matta, M., (2014). A Body of Dissatisfaction: A Study of the Effects of Media Imperialism in Kuwait. *American Journal of Humanities and Social Sciences*, 2, (1), 2014, 76-87

Murray, J. P. (2008). Media violence the effects are both real and strong. *American Behavioral Scientist*, 51(8), 1212-1230.

Myers, D. G. (2013). The Self in a Social World. In D. G. Myers (Author), *Social Psychology* (11th ed., p. 40). New York, NY: McGraw Hill.

O'Keeffe, G. S., & Clarke-Pearson, K. (2011). The impact of social media on children, adolescents, and families. *Pediatrics*, 127(4), 800-804

Olimat, Muhamad S. "Women and politics in Kuwait." *Journal of International Women's studies* 11.2 (2009): 199-212.

Olson, S. (2014, June 25). Misery Loves Company (So Stop Trying To Cheer Me Up). *Medical Daily*.Retrieved 26 June 2014 from <http://www.medicaldaily.com/low-self-esteem-sufferers-prefer-negative-comments-so-dont-cheer-them-289936>.

Perse, E., & Lambert. J (2016). Media Effects and Society. New York: Routledge.

Phinney, J. S. (1991). Ethnic identity and self-esteem: A review and integration. *Hispanic Journal of Behavioral Sciences, 13 (2)*, 193-208.

Rubin, A. (2002). The uses-and-gratifications perspective of media effects. In J. Bryant & D. Zillmann (Eds.), Media effects: Advances in theory and research (2nd ed., pp. 525-548). Hillsdale, NJ: Lawrence Erlbaum Associates, Inc.

Salem, F., &Mourtada, R. (2011). Facebook Usage: Factors and ANALYSIS. 1(1). Retrieved from http://www.arabsocialmediareport.com/UserManagement PDF/ASMR Report 1.pdf

Shao, G. (2009). Understanding the appeal of user-generated media: a uses and gratification perspective. *Internet research*, *19*(1), 7-25.

Sheldon, P., & Bryant, K. (2016). Instagram: Motives for its use and relationship to narcissism and contextual age. *Computers in Human Behavior*, *58*, 89-97.

Smith, M. (1999). "E-merging strategies of identity: the rhetorical construction of self in personal web sites", doctoral dissertation, Ohio University, Athens, OH.

Stafford, T. F., Stafford, M. R., & Schkade, L. L. (2004). Determining uses and gratifications for the Internet. *Decision sciences*, *35*(2), 259-288.

Stanger, N., Alnaghaimshi, N., & Pearson, E. (2017). How do Saudi youth engage with social media?. *First Monday, 22*(5).

Statista. (2014). Instagram monthly active users 2014. Retrieved April 1, 2015, from http://www.statista.com/statistics/253577/number-of-monthly-active-instagram-users/

Sultan, A. L. (2011). *The Impact of Customer Relationship Marketing in The Luxury Retail Market of Kuwait: A Thematic Analysis* (Doctoral dissertation, University of Gloucestershire).

Tétreault, M. A., & Al-Mughni, H. (1995). Modernization and its discontents: State and gender in Kuwait. *The Middle East Journal*, 403-417.

Tétreault, M. A. (2001). A state of two minds: State cultures, women, and politics in Kuwait. *International Journal of Middle East Studies*, *33*(2), 203-220.

Theocharis, Y., & Quintelier, E. (2016). Stimulating citizenship or expanding entertainment? The effect of Facebook on adolescent participation. *New media & society*, *18*(5), 817-836.

Totems. (14 January 2014). Retrieved October 7, 2014, from http://totems.co/blog/gender-instagram-infographic/

Toumi, H. (2015, July 5). Kuwait to deport expatriates found to be behind rumours. *Gulf News*. Retrieved July 13, 2015 from http://gulfnews.com/news/gulf/kuwait/kuwait-to-deport-expatriates-found-to-be-behind-rumours-1.1545514

Trammell, K. and Keshelashvili, A. (2005). Examining the new influencers: a self-presentation study of a-list blogs. *Journalism & Mass Communication Quarterly*, Vol. 82 No. 4, pp. 968-82.

University of North Carolina at Pembroke. (n.d.). *The Brief History of Social Media*. Retrieved June 13, 2014, from http://www2.uncp.edu/home/acurtis/NewMedia/SocialMedia/SocialMediaHistory.html

Urista, M. A., Dong, Q., & Day, K. D. (2009). Explaining why young adults use MySpace and Facebook through uses and gratifications theory. *Human Communication*, *12*(2), 215-229

USA Today. (2005, May 16). Kuwait approves women's political rights. Retrieved from http://usatoday30.usatoday.com/news/world/2005-05-16-kuwait-women_x.htm
http://usatoday30.usatoday.com/news/world/2005-05-16-kuwait-women_x.htm

Vaknin, S.(n.d.). Narcissistic Rage and Narcissistic Injury: The Intermittent Explosive Narcissist. Retrieved June 24, 2014, from http://samvak.tripod.com/journal86.html
http://samvak.tripod.com/journal86.html

Victoria, S.D. (n.d.). How to Spot a Narcissist - World of Psychology. *Psych Central*. Retrieved June 24, 2014, from http://psychcentral.com/blog/archives/2008/08/04/how-to-spot-a-narcissist/
http://psychcentral.com/blog/archives/2008/08/04/how-to-spot-a-narcissist/

Wheeler, D. (2000). New Media, Globalization and Kuwaiti National Identity. *Middle East Journal*, 54(3), 432-444. Retrieved from JSTOR database

Wheeler, D. (2003). The Internet and Youth Subculture in Kuwait. *Journal of Computer-Mediated Communication*.8 (2) Retrieved from JSTOR database

Appendix

Rosenberg Self-Esteem Scale

The scale is a ten-item Likert scale with items answered on a four-point scale - from strongly agree to strongly disagree. The original sample for which the scale was developed consisted of 5,024 High School Juniors and Seniors from 10 randomly selected schools in New York State.

Instructions: Below is a list of statements dealing with your general feelings about yourself. If you strongly agree, circle SA. If you agree with the statement, circle A. If you disagree, circle D. If you strongly disagree, circle SD.

1.	On the whole, I am satisfied with myself.	SA	A	D	SD
2.	At times, I think I am no good at all.	SA	A	D	SD
3.	I feel that I have a number of good qualities.	SA	A	D	SD
4.	I am able to do things as well as most other people.	SA	A	D	SD
5.	*I feel I do not have much to be proud of.	SA	A	D	SD
6.	*I certainly feel useless at times.	SA	A	D	SD
7.	I feel that I'm a person of worth, at least on an equal plane with others.	SA	A	D	SD
8.	*I wish I could have more respect for myself.	SA	A	D	SD
9.	*All in all, I am inclined to feel that I am a failure.	SA	A	D	SD
10.	I take a positive attitude toward myself.	SA	A	D	SD

Scoring: SA=3, A=2, D=1, SD=0. Items with an asterisk are reverse scored, that is, SA=0, A=1, D=2, SD=3. Sum the scores for the 10 items. The higher the score, the higher the self-esteem.

The scale may be used without explicit permission. The author's family, however, would like to be kept informed of its use:

The Morris Rosenberg Foundation c/o Department of Sociology University of

Maryland 2112 Art/Soc Building

College Park, MD 20742-1315 References

References with further characteristics of the scale:

Crandal, R. (1973). The measurement of self-esteem and related constructs, Pp. 80-82 in J.P.Robinson & P.R.Shaver (Eds), Measures of social psychological attitudes.Revised edition. Ann Arbor: ISR.

Rosenberg, M. (1965). Society and the adolescent self-image. Princeton, NJ: Princeton University Press.

Wylie, R. C. (1974). The self-concept. Revised edition. Lincoln, Nebraska: University of Nebraska Press.

NPI-16

Read each pair of statements below and place an "X" by the one that comes closest to describing your feelings and beliefs about yourself. You may feel that neither statement describes you well but pick the one that comes closest. **Please complete all pairs**.

1. __ I really like to be the center of attention
   __ It makes me uncomfortable to be the center of attention

2. __ I am no better or no worse than most people
   __ I think I am a special person

3. __ Everybody likes to hear my stories
   __ Sometimes I tell good stories

4. __ I usually get the respect that I deserve
   __ I insist upon getting the respect that is due me

5. __ I don't mind following orders
   __ I like having authority over people

6. __ I am going to be a great person
   __ I hope I am going to be successful

7. __ People sometimes believe what I tell them
   __ I can make anybody believe anything I want them to

8. __ I expect a great deal from other people
   __ I like to do things for other people

9 __ I like to be the center of attention
 __ I prefer to blend in with the crowd

10 __ I am much like everybody else
 __ I am an extraordinary person

11 __ I always know what I am doing
 __ Sometimes I am not sure of what I am doing

12 __ I don't like it when I find myself manipulating people
 __ I find it easy to manipulate people

13 __ Being an authority doesn't mean that much to me
 __ People always seem to recognize my authority

14 __ I know that I am good because everybody keeps telling me so
 __ When people compliment me, I sometimes get embarrassed

15 __ I try not to be a showoff
 __ I am apt to show off if I get the chance

16 __ I am more capable than other people
 __ There is a lot that I can learn from other people

NPI-16 Key: Responses consistent with narcissism are shown in bold.

1 __ **I really like to be the center of attention**
 __ It makes me uncomfortable to be the center of attention

2 __ I am no better or nor worse than most people
 __ **I think I am a special person**

3 __ **Everybody likes to hear my stories**
  __ Sometimes I tell good stories

4 __ I usually get the respect that I deserve
  __ **I insist upon getting the respect that is due me**

5 __ I don't mind following orders
  __ **I like having authority over people**

6 __ **I am going to be a great person**
  __ I hope I am going to be successful

7 __ People sometimes believe what I tell them
  __ **I can make anybody believe anything I want them to**

8 __ **I expect a great deal from other people**
  __ I like to do things for other people

9 __ **I like to be the center of attention**
  __ I prefer to blend in with the crowd

10 __ I am much like everybody else
   __ **I am an extraordinary person**

11 __ **I always know what I am doing**
   __ Sometimes I am not sure of what I am doing

12 __ I don't like it when I find myself manipulating people
   __ **I find it easy to manipulate people**

13 __ Being an authority doesn't mean that much to me
   __ **People always seem to recognize my authority**

14 __ **I know that I am good because everybody keeps telling me so**
   __ When people compliment me, I sometimes get embarrassed

15 __ I try not to be a showoff
   __ **I am apt to show off if I get the chance**

16 __ **I am more capable than other people**
   __ There is a lot that I can learn from other people

Scoring: compute proportion of responses consistent with narcissism.

Background: The NPI-16 items are drawn from across the dimensions of Raskin and Terry's (1988) 40-item measure. Relevant references are noted below:

Ames, Daniel R., Rose, Paul, and Anderson, Cameron P. (2006). The NPI-16 as a short measure of narcissism. *Journal of Research in Personality, 40,* 440-450.

Raskin, R., & Terry, H. (1988). A principal-components analysis of the Narcissistic Personality Inventory and further evidence of its construct validity. *Journal of Personality and Social Psychology, 54,* 890–902.

http://www.psychologytoday.com/blog/fulfillment-any-age/201201/the-healthy-side-narcissism

CHAPTER 4

Coping Mechanism

THE QUEST FOR a social identity is continuous and forever evolving as youth become exposed to various life situations and new experiences, where they must take control of their decisions and how they react to the given circumstances. What we will be examining in this section is the coping strategies and mechanism through a gender lens in a collectivist society, along with cases of resilience and overcoming adversaries in the recent times, especially during the COVID-19 pandemic which started in earlier 2020. Youth and young adults in Kuwait have demonstrated varying coping skills to manage stress, when compared to other countries and societies. The people of Kuwait, as illustrated previously, are subsidized by the government in various life essential functions, which has allowed them to be continuously dependent and secure. Aside from the Gulf war in 1990, Kuwait did not face any major stressful events at large, therefore understanding how the people are developing resilience and what coping mechanisms they employ in challenging times hasn't been researched widely and we look to shed some light on this phenomenon. Since the youth sample examined and studied in this collection of researches have not experienced the Gulf war with an adult mindset, we are considering different modules including Psychological Immune System, Biopsychosocial, Self-Esteem, and varying coping skills theories to be outlines in the next chapter to be able to draw conclusions on how the youth build their resilience and develop their coping mechanism. Similarly, we look at some of the coping skills developed, especially through the peak of the pandemic, to further understand how collectivist societies compared to individualist societies prompt building resilience against stressful situations, and how this overall juxtaposition further influences an individual's social identity building. The youth's identities examined reveal the societal and cultural effects intertwined in their social identity construction, and how adversaries could present an opportunity to further reflect on one's internal identity against external identities, which are illustrated in social settings, both offline and online.

As published in Athens Journal of Mediterranean Studies – Volume 8, Issue 1, January 2021 – Pages 49-66.

Navigating Through Resilience: Young Adults in Kuwait

By Juliet Dinkha, Aya Abdulhadi, Ayshah Al-Kandari & Saja Al-Obaid

Abstract

Individual's behaviors, mindset and personality is greatly affected by their social circle and shaped by their past experiences, leading individuals to develop resilience against stressful situations and adversaries. Such situations are mainly experienced during adolescence stage presenting an opportunity to understand how individuals think they will react to stressful times and what measures do they consider if and when crises hit. The inevitable goal of the research is to find out how and if individuals build resilience to negative situations and find themselves to express and feel happiness instead of succumbing to negative emotions and behaviors. For a better understanding of their self-resilience, we created a framework of Internal and External Resilience to guide us with the findings. This research was conducted during the early stage of the COVID-19 spread, which did not present to be a pandemic at the time and hadn't affected one's life as gravely. In gathering our research, questions that will be kept in mind but are not limited to, include: how do two individuals who experience similar situations react in different ways, one negatively affected left while the other unaffected? Do past experiences make individuals more resilient to situations that they came into contact with? With those probing questions, we would be able to further understand the relationship between building resilience and experiencing hopelessness in times of crises.

Keywords: Resilience; Adversaries; Crises; Hopelessness; Psychological Immune System

Introduction

In physical science, resilience is the capacity of a strained body to recover its size and shape after some deformation caused by compressive stress. In psychology, resilience may be thought of as the process of functioning as well or better than unstressed individuals in the face of adversity. In other words, resilience is the capacity for an individual to overcome stressful and difficult situations that may arise in life. This topic of study came about when researchers realized that there were some people who "worked well, played well, loved well, and expected well" despite major stresses (Werner & Smith, 1992, p. 262). Resilience, then, requires two conditions: (1) the person must be, now or in the past, exposed to adversity, and (2) the person must be doing well. Resilience requires that young adults be exposed to *adversity, stress, or risk*. A risk factor is any individual or environmental characteristic that increases the likelihood of some negative outcome. Our research would like to uncover how individuals react to situations they are put into based on their past experiences, trauma or personal difficulties. The aim is to find out how happiness is expressed or on the contrary, how happiness is not being expressed, in individuals who have had tough pasts. Similar to the glass half full or half empty concept, we would be able to deduce if some negative situations can impact individuals in different ways.

In the article "Relationship of Resilience to Personality, Coping, and Psychiatric Symptoms in Young Adults" resilience is typically seen less in children whom have been exposed to disadvantages and trauma (Campbell-Sills, et al., 2006). With regards to children exposed to traumatic experiences it has been found that when they have higher exposure to trauma they manifest higher levels of psychiatric symptoms and lower levels of resilience. The level of resilience in children and adolescents is associated with certain personality traits and characteristics they have as well as the type of coping mechanism they use to deal with stressors. In addition to one's personality and coping techniques, one's resiliency levels vary depending on how they view the world and the stressful events they experience. Whether one looks at an experience with a positive outlook or a negative outlook, the levels of their resilience will vary. Resilience is said to be higher in individuals who have close relationships with friends/family and have a positive outlook on negative situations. Whereas individuals who don't have close friends/family relationships and have a pessimistic outlook, are more prone to exhibiting less resilience when faced with adversaries.

The age of 18-25 is a crucial phase in one's life, as it is the time where individuals graduate from high school or university or are pursuing their career. This period is filled with stress and emotional burnouts, which is why this age range is very important to study and understand how they practice resilience. According to Ong, Bergeman, Bisconti, and Wallace (2006), one way in which resilience is practiced is through the adaptation and maintenance of positive outcomes towards stressful events (Ong, et al., 2006, p. 730). As it was discovered that stressful events cause negative emotions, thus adaptation and perseverance would invoke positive emotions (Ong, et al., 2006, p. 731). Nonetheless, resilience is found to have a contribution in the process of strengthening resistance to and recovery from stress (Ong, et al., 2006 p. 731).

Literature Review

Resilience is illustrated by Gooding, Hurst, Johnson and Tarrier as a protective or in other words defense mechanism for stressors (Gooding, et al., 2011, p. 262). In young adults, resilience seems to be related to social support, this is understandable as at this age, people tend to create relationships and social ties outside their familial circle (Gooding, et al., 2011, p. 262). According to Gooding et al. there are predictors for psychological resilience which are "emotional health and well-being, self-rated successful ageing, social contact with family and friends, optimism and a lack of cognitive failures" (Gooding, et al., 2011, pp. 262-263). Therefore, people who score low in the hopelessness scale will undoubtedly have greater resilience, as tough times would bring out their coping skills (Gooding, et al., 2011, p. 262).

Nevertheless, there are protective factors that bestow resilience. Some of which are characteristics developed throughout the individual's life.

According to Lereya et al., those include and are not limited to positive characteristics, self-control, empathy, intelligence, self-esteem and problem-solving skills (Lereya, et al., 2016, pp. 1-2). Environments also play a huge role, such as environments both in the familial circle and outside of it, examples are functional family relationships and a supportive environment outside the family (Lereya, et al., 2016, p. 2). This is important as having a support system, whether it's a family member or members or friends or teachers, can help boost an individual's confidence and the idea that they have someone to fall back onto (Lereya, et al., 2016, p. 2). Functional family relationships create positive development and subsequently help them cope with stressful events (Lereya, et al., 2016, p. 2). As for outside the family, a supportive environment whether it be in schools, workplace or even between friends is recognized to be a possible protective factor against stressors (Lereya, et al., 2016, p. 2).

Research conducted by Atsushi Oshio et al. focused on the measurement of resilience in adolescence as significant psychological and social changes occur throughout that time period and the outcome of coming into contact with those adversities will indicate factors of resilience in the individual (Oshi, et al., 2003, p. 1217). In their article, Atsushi Oshio et al. used a multitude of scales designed to assess the construct validity of the Adolescent Resilience Scale (Oshi, et al., 2003, p. 1218). They hypothesized that resilient adolescent individuals (ages 19 to 23) are capable to maintain a positive mental health even after experiencing adversities and painful life experiences (Oshi, et al., 2003, p. 1218). Their findings show that resilience scores did not have any connection to experiencing negative life events, however there was a relationship between resilience and general health (Oshi, et al., 2003, p. 1219). As well as, a relationship between negative life events and general health (Oshi, et al., 2003, p. 1219). Their research showed that adolescent resilience score indicates features that exhibit resilience after experiencing negative events in life, which led them to conclude the validity of the Adolescent Resilience Scale (Oshi, et al., 2003, p. 1221). The authors explained that further studies should be conducted to further identify information on the psychological recovery process of individuals whose features of resilience were identified through the Adolescent Resilience Scale.

Modules

Understanding how one's brain leads and supports our cognitive selves through difficult times can be derived from numerous behavioral and psychology modules. These modules explain how the human brain reacts to trauma, learns from trauma and how to cope with it and with potential similar situations, with the main objective of protecting us from further trauma, thus forming coping mechanism through resilience. Such behaviors are greatly affected by the individual's outlook about life, self-belief, self-esteem and capabilities, in addition to how they perceive their role as part of their social circle. For the purpose of our study, we will be deucing the results based on the following modules:

Psychological Immune System (PIS)

Just like how our immune system defeats invading cells, we have a psychological one. Psychological immune system in other words is the mental defense system. We can define psychological immune system as "an integrated system of cognitive, motivational and behavioral personality dimensions that should provide immunity against stress, promote healthy development and serve as stress resistance resources or psychological antibodies" (Dubey & Shahi, 2011, p. 37). Similarly to our immune system once our body identifies the invading cells and how to protect us from it, our brain functions in the same approach. Once our brain has experienced stress or other mental threats, our brain will know how to deal with it in a way that does not harm us, and thus our mental health will potentially improve and help us adapt (Bóna, 2014, p. 14). Our brain knows how to deal with such events through the knowledge gained from previous exposure of stressors (Bóna, 2014, p. 15). Thus, our mind becomes and is adapted to better resilience post stressful event.

Biopsychosocial

Biopsychosocial is a model that illustrates how biological, psychological and social factors determine why someone acts in a certain way or suffer from a certain disorder or how they developed throughout their life. This theory indicates but is not limited to the idea that an individual's social environment, biological makeup, and psyche encourage how they would act in certain occasions. In the face of stressors, an individual's resilience is influenced by their biopsychosocial. Especially the social environment, as social environment has a huge impact on how someone deals with stressors, whether someone has a secure social environment or not, and that would influence their psychological response.

Self-Esteem

Self-esteem can be defined as your opinion about yourself and your self-worth. One's self-esteem can come from one's experiences and interpersonal relationships with others. Just by simply saying self-esteem is a broad word, it is important to note that self-esteem has a scale spectrum. Individuals can fall on different ends on the spectrum and will have different outcomes and effects in their personal lives (Mruk, 2006, p. 2). Disorders such as depression and anxiety are likely develop in individuals who possess a low self-esteem. There is also a middle spectrum which can affect how an individual cope with failure, losses or any other problems that they may be facing (Mruk, 2006, p. 2). Individuals who have higher self-esteem are more likely to believe that they can overcome any obstacle they face. They are more compassionate towards themselves and others which will in return make them capable of being resilient. Those individuals will be able to deal with stressful stressors and have the ability to problem solve and persevere through adversities.

Hypotheses

1. If individuals scale high on their hopelessness levels then that will lead to a decrease in resiliency.

2. If individuals scale high on resiliency then they would indicate better coping skills for managing stress.

3. High levels of positive emotions increases the chance for one to maintain and have resilience during stressful times.

Method

For our research we picked two set of questionnaires that would provide us with answers to our hypotheses and determine their validity. The first was the Beck Hopelessness Scale (BHS) which is a questionnaire of 20 true or false questions that was developed by Dr. Aaron T. Beck (Beck, 1988). The questionnaire was developed for adults ages 17 and above, to measure aspects of hopelessness like having feelings about the future, loss of motivation, and expectations, to the extent of indicating suicidal attempts in depressed people (Beck, 1988). Moving on to the second scale used in our research which is a 28 item questionnaire, which was developed to measure resilience in adults called "The Resilience Research Centre Adult Resilience Measure (RRC-ARM)" scale. The RRC-ARM questionnaire has different sections, each caters a certain data collection method, in our case we picked Section C option 2, that is a three-point response scale, which is an easier reading level, as the scale is administered to individuals whose primary language is Arabic. We have also used Section A from the RRC-ARM, which are some basic questions used to introduce the recipient to us, by providing a few key information about themselves, such as their nationality, gender, age and so on. This is very important, as those questions give us the advantage of knowing certain aspects about our sample, in order to be able to deduce further understanding of their behaviors.

As for the means of distributing our questionnaire, we decided to opt for a more efficient method that could reach a vast number of individuals and at a fast pace, which is by creating an electronic questionnaire using surveymonkey.com, and dispersing it electronically. A hyperlink was developed in order to easily send it out to people instead of using emails or handing out physical questionnaire papers. Once the hyperlink is clicked, participants would be directed to a landing page which displayed the survey. By following this method, we ensured that people can easily receive the hyperlink, and are able to answer the questionnaire wherever and whenever they decide to do so. In addition to this being flexible on when and where they can complete the survey, it can also be distributed by those who have already completed it and want to share it with others whom they think could complete the survey as well. One of the advantages of having an electronic survey is that once an individual has completed the survey on a specific device, they cannot attempt to take the survey again on the same device. This is due to the website being able to recognize their device's IP address, limiting individuals from answering the survey more than once.

Our survey was answered by 130 respondents, and all their data were collected by surveymoneky.com and were accessible for the research team to analyze. Utilizing some of the basic results analysis features available on the website, charts pertaining to our sample's demographics were created to support with our further understanding of the selected questionnaire results and relationship between hopelessness and resilience. The research team cross checked the automated charts created to ensure all answers received were accounted for and included in the results tables, as shared in the following section.

[blinded], Navigating Through Resilience: Young Adults in Kuwait, this study didn't seek any approval by an internal review board because this process is not applied in the affiliated university nor followed in this region. We are not bound to receive reviews by any committee when conducting researches, however, the research is shared internally with colleagues for feedback and to keep the department Chair updated on the research projects.

RESULTS

Table 1. Age Group

Categories	Responses (percentage)
Under 18	2.00%
18-25	84.00%
Above 25	14.00%
Total	100%

Table 2. Gender

Categories	Results (Percentage)
Male	22%
Female	78%
Total	100%

Table 3. Educational Level

Categories	Results (percentage)
High School Diploma	44.00%
College Degree	9.00%
Bachelor Degree	41.00%
Master Degree	6.00%
Doctorate Degree	0.00%
Total	100%

Table 4. Household

Categories	Results (Percentage)
Mother	17.17%
Father	8.08%
Grandparents	0.00%
Aunts/Uncles	1.01%
Cousins	0.00%
Friends	0.00%
Siblings	1.01%
Nuclear family (your parents and siblings)	68.69%
Alone	4.04%
Total:	100%

Table 5. Moving Houses

Categories	Results (percentage)
Once	16.16%
Twice	15.15%
Three times	6.06%
Four times	4.04%
None	58.59%
Total	100%

Table 6. Nationality

Categories	Results (Percentage)
Kuwaiti	76.00%
Specify if non Kuwaiti	24.00%
Total	100.00%

Table 7. Beck Hopelessness Scale Questionnaire

Categories	True	False
I look forward to the future with hope and enthusiasm.	84.85%	15.15%
I might as well give up because there is nothing I can do about making things better for myself.	16.00%	84.00%
When things are going badly, I am helped by knowing that they cannot stay that way forever.	84.00%	16.00%
I can't imagine what my life would be like in ten years.	68.00%	32.00%
I have enough time to accomplish the things I want to do.	70.71%	29.29%
In the future, I expect to succeed in what concerns me most.	87.88%	12.12%
My future seems dark to me.	22.22%	77.78%
I happen to be particularly lucky, and I expect to get more of the good things in life like than the average person.	63.00%	37%
I just can't get the breaks, and there is no reason I will in the future.	25.25%	74.75%
My past experiences have prepared me well for the future.	80.81%	19.19%
All I can see ahead of me is unpleasantness rather than pleasantness.	14.29%	85.71%
I don't expect to get what I really want.	48.48%	51.52%
When I look ahead to the future, I expect that I will be happier than I am now.	82.83%	17.17%

Things just won't work out the way I want them to.	41.41%	58.59%
I have great faith in the future.	76.77%	23.23%
I never get what I want, so it's foolish to want anything.	13.13%	86.87%
It's very unlikely that I will get any real satisfaction in the future.	20.20%	79.80%
The future seems vague and uncertain to me.	52.53%	47.47%
I can look forward to more good times than bad times.	88.89%	11.11%
There's no use in really trying to get anything I want because I probably won't get it.	14.29%	85.71%

Table 8. RRC-ARM Questionnaire

	No	Sometimes	Yes
I have people in my life who I can respect	1.00%	11.00%	88.00%
I share/cooperate with people around me	2.00%	43.00%	55.00%
Getting and improving qualifications and skills is important to me	3.00%	17.00%	80.00%
I know how to behave in different social situations (such as at work, home, or other public places)	6.00%	18.00%	76.00%
My family is supportive towards me	8.00%	35.00%	57.00%
My family Knows a lot about me (for example, who my friends are, what I like to do)	17.00%	39.00%	44.00%

COPING MECHANISM

If I am hungry, I can usually get enough food to eat.	5.00%	15.00%	80.00%
I try to finish activities that I start.	2.00%	38.00%	60.00%
Spiritual beliefs are a source of strength for me (for example, believing in God or Allah)	5.00%	20.00%	75.00%
I am proud of my ethnic background (for example, I am proud of where my family comes from or know a lot about my family's history).	4.00%	17.00%	79.00%
People think that I am fun to be with.	9.00%	34.00%	57.00%
I talk to my family/partner about how I feel (for example, when I am sad or concerned)	27.00%	48.00%	25.00%
When things don't go my way, I usually fix it without hurting myself or other people (e.g. without using drugs or being violent)	7.00%	19.00%	74.00%
I feel supported by my friends	7.00%	39.00%	54.00%
I know where to go if I need help	14.00%	36.00%	50.00%
I feel that I belong in my community	30.00%	35.00%	35.00%
My family cares about me when times are hard (for example, when I am ill or in trouble)	3.00%	22.00%	75.00%
My Friends cares about me when times are hard (for example, when I am ill or in trouble)	10.00%	28.00%	62.00%

I am treated fairly	9.00%	48.00%	43.00%
I have opportunities to show others that I can act responsibly	6.00%	28.00%	66.00%
I know what I am good at	2.00%	35.00%	63.00%
I participate in religious activities (like going to church or mosque)	33.00%	42.00%	25.00%
I think it is important to help out in my community	5.00%	21.00%	74.00%
I feel secure when I am with my family	11.00%	31.00%	58.00%
I have opportunities to apply my abilities in life (like using skills, working at a job, or caring for others)	7.00%	33.00%	60.00%
I like my family's culture and the way my family celebrates things (e.g. holidays)	8.00%	35.00%	57.00%
I like my community's culture and the way my community celebrates things (e.g. holidays or festivals)	9.00%	43.00%	48.00%

Table 9. Social Support Circle (*Responses were categorized together based on similarities*)

Categories	Results (In numbers)
Family (including both parents, siblings, and cousins)	21
Mother	13
Father	3
Friends	18
Family and Friends	25
No one	11
Partners	2
Myself	2

Discussion

This research studied if individuals in Kuwait are capable of building up resilience to negative situations and what type of coping skills they employ to manage stress, in response to the RRC-ARM questionnaire and the Beck Hopelessness Scale (BHS) questionnaire. Our results proposed a high level of resilience, leading us to create a framework to understand the individual's resilience through Internal and External Resilience modules that we are presenting in this paper. For the purpose of this analysis, Internal Resilience is used to refer to how individuals are resilient, while External Resilience refers to how they think they are resilient. Both terms will form the basis to understand the results of our sample and how their responses to the RRC-ARM and BHS questionnaires correlate with resilience.

While we look at our sample at large, 76% of whom are Kuwaitis, the majority of our respondents live with their nuclear family, consisting of their parents and siblings, and since Kuwait is a collectivist society, it is expected that family members stay together until they get married, and in some cases, the males in the family remain to live with their parents and start their own family at their parent's house. Additionally, 58.59% of our sample have been living in the same house and haven't moved, which denotes a form of family stability as well and aids in raising a resilient personality, which will continue to seek social stability.

Therefore, and in response to our hypothesis (H1), individuals scored low on their hopelessness levels leading to high levels of resiliency. Whether this resiliency is truly an internal form of resilience or not, could only be dependent on the individual's experience during times of crises. About 80.81% of our sample believe that their past experiences have prepared them well for the future. Certain stressful situations are redundant in one's life, in which previous experiences aid in how one copes with new stressful situations they are faced with. This enforces the Psychological Immune System (PIS) module, which creates 'an integrated system of cognitive, motivational and behavioral personality dimensions that should provide immunity against stress, promote healthy development and serve as stress resistance resources or psychological antibodies' (Dubey & Shahi, 2011, p. 37). Thus increasing their resiliency level and belief that they are and capable of being resilient.

Based on our results (see Table 8), we can deduce that our respondents have a high resiliency and as speculated in our hypothesis (H2), this indicates that they have better coping skills for managing stress. Receiving social support from family members and understanding one's actions and consequences, capabilities and role in the community, supports the individual in being resilient in the face of advertise and increases their internal resilience. A solid support system with an open and trusted relationship with family and friends, whom individuals can count on in times of need, does create a higher sense of internal resilience.

Our sample is raised by a generation that is most likely to have had experienced the Gulf war in 1990, thus their parents must have instilled the notion of resiliency in them in order to prepare them to face stressful situations that they might encounter. Another stress-coping skill deduced from the results is intertwined with strong religious beliefs and receiving spiritual support, as agreed by 75% of our sample, leading them to cope with stressful times and overcome them with the belief of attaining a better outcome and future, thus increasing their external resilience. It is only during a stressful encounter that we could test their resilience and understand if it is also an internal form of resilience that is exhibited by individuals or not.

Additionally, violence is not considered as a first resort during stressful times, according to 74% of our respondents. This correlates with the fact that 78% of our respondents are females, and they are more likely be more considerate of their actions. The reason being is that given the collectivist nature of the Kuwaiti society, and how their actions are influenced by their social standing and family name, the females would try to maintain their families' reputation thus limit any violent acts. Other coping skills as indicated by our sample are linked to measures taken by individuals who often break on a personal and social level, and resort to measures such as crying, anger or denial to try and cope with the stressful situations they are presented with. Those individuals are more likely to present internal resilience, as they would be a better predictor of how resilient they truly are.

Our sample believes that they have acquired certain social skills and qualifications and are able to compete, grow, evolve and control their behaviors at different social situations. Being respected by family and the community, and maintaining a certain social status and stability do correlate positively with being able to stay resilient, thus proves our hypothesis (H3) to be true. It is also worth noting that positive emotions about the future self, and especially to our Kuwaiti sample, could be linked to receiving support from the government, thus feeling safe and more hopeful, as indicated by 84.85% our respondents in Table 7. The cultural instinct is to protect its people against stressors, therefore people may see this protection as a form of self-resilience. Being certain of having a set of privileges and the rightful access to a number of essential resources including healthcare, education, finance and social support, provides a sense of a better future and creates a positive outlook, thus leading individuals to build resilience within.

Due to the nature of the privilege system in Kuwait, individuals think that they are prepared for the future. However, one could argue that they are poor predictors of their feelings as they have not experienced true resilience, therefore they think that they are resilient or able to become resilient, which is the form of external resilience. Kuwait, when compared globally, where individuals are subjected to stressors such as losing one's job, finding adequate housing, poor healthcare or unclear future endeavors and instability is experienced, individuals true self resilience is exhibited. Only then that individuals would be a more accurate predictors of their resilient self, because they have lived through a stressful situation and would be able to deduce their preparedness and ability to cope with it or not.

The contradictions in some of the results we received could be due to the responses received from the expatriates, around 24% of our sample, who do not necessarily have access to the same privilege system as Kuwaitis, but could also be based on feedback from the Kuwaitis who don't feel safe in their own home and don't trust the system in general. This hopelessness and low self-resilience is possibly experienced by those individuals who lack a strong social support system with dysfunctional family, thus losing the hope and the need to be resilient.

Most of our sample exhibited external resilience throughout the results, and this could be due to the fact that this study was conducted during the beginning of a pandemic crises, where Kuwait wasn't closely touched by its repercussions. Whereas, we would expect to see more of internal resilience exhibited and a true measure of resilience as the pandemic unfolds and individuals are impacted.

Limitations

The language used for the questionnaire

When looking at some of the discrepancies in the results, they could be due to a number of limitations our study encountered in hindsight which are also dependent on the sample that answered our questionnaire. Language barrier could be one of the main limitations we had faced, as the questionnaires were circulated in the English language and most of the respondents' first language is Arabic. It could be that some participants may have not understood the questions correctly, thus not providing us with the correct representation of their feelings and understanding of resilience.

Fear of confidentially breach

A second limitation could be due to the sensitivity of the subject, and the type of the questions posed, although it was highlighted that the participation is confidential, respondents maybe have felt vulnerable to share true accounts of past experiences or to reflect on their true selves, thus not sharing accurate representations in their answers and trying to show they are better than they truly are.

The time of conducting the study outside the spike of a crisis

The time in which the study was conducted was during the early stages of the pandemic of COVID-19, where most respondents could have shared their hopeful perception of their resilient self, whereas as the pandemic expanded, their responses would have been actually different. If the study were conducted during the spike of the pandemic, and the respondents were actually subjected to repercussions of the situations and the radical changes which later came into effect while answering the questionnaires, we would expect the results to reflect a better measure of internal resilience as opposed to external resilience, which we believe is mainly exhibited by the respondents.

The age of the participants

Moreover, the current sample examined, not only that they may have not gone through stressors but they are a generation that is more stable financially and are yielding the hard work and efforts of their parents, thus they are less likely to understand what true resilience is. Our age group could have been expanded to include an older population who were more likely to have experienced stressors themselves and not only have heard of such situations from their parents or grandparents. Such stories from close social groups can influence the individual's behaviors and perceptions more likely compared to historical account of events that doesn't relate to the individual, however, they would not be contributing to a true resilience measure if they weren't subjected to test their resilience.

References

Beck A.T. (1988). "Beck Hopelessness Scale." The Psychological Corporation.

Bóna, K. (2014). "An exploration of the psychological immune system in Hungarian gymnasts." University of Jyväskylä.

Campbell-Sills, L., Cohan, S. L., & Stein, M. B. (2006). Relationship of resilience to personality, coping, and psychiatric symptoms in young adults. Behaviour Research and Therapy, 44(4), 585–599.

Dubey, A., & Shahi, D. (2011) Psychological immunity and coping strategies: A study on medical professionals. Indian Journal of Social Science Researches, 8 (1-2), 36-47.

Lereya, S. T., Humphrey, N., Patalay, P., Wolpert, M., Böhnke, J. R., Macdougall, A., & Deighton, J. (2016). "The student resilience survey: psychometric validation and associations with mental health. *Child and Adolescent Psychiatry and Mental Health"*, *10*(1), 1–2. doi: 10.1186/s13034-016-0132-5

Mruk, Christopher J. *Self-Esteem Research, Theory, and Practice: toward a Positive Psychology of Self-Esteem*. Springer, 2006.

Ong, A. D., Bergeman, C. S., Bisconti, T. L., & Wallace, K. A. (2006). "Psychological resilience, positive emotions, and successful adaptation to stress in later life". *Journal of Personality and Social Psychology,91*(4), 730-749. doi:10.1037/0022-3514.91.4.730

Oshio, A., Kaneko, H., Nagamine, S., & Nakaya, M. (2003). Construct Validity Of The Adolescent Resilience Scale. *Psychological Reports, 93*(7), 1217–1222. doi: 10.2466/pr0.93.7.1217-1222

The Resilience Research Centre Adult Resilience Measure (RRC-ARM), Resilience Research Center, Canada, 2016.

Werner, E. E., & Smith, R.S. (1992). Overcoming the odds: High-risk children from birth to adulthood. Ithaca, NY: Cornell University Press

Appendix
Survey for a Research Paper

1. Age?
    a. Under 18
    b. 18-25
    c. Above 25

2. Gender?
    a. Female
    b. Male

3. What is the highest level of education you have completed?
    a. High School Diploma
    b. College Diploma
    c. Bachelor Degree
    d. Master Degree
    e. Doctorate Degree

4. Who do you live with?
    a. Mother
    b. Father
    c. Grandparents
    d. Aunts/Uncles
    e. Cousins
    f. Friends
    g. Siblings
    h. Nuclear Family (your parents and siblings)
    i. Alone

5. How many times have you moved homes in the past 5 years?
    a. Once
    b. Twice
    c. Three times

d. Four times
   e. None

6. Please indicate who you consider to be your social support?
   (Text box)

7. To which of the following groups do you belong?
   a. Kuwaiti
   b. Specify if not Kuwaiti

8. Please answer the following true or false questions.
   a. I look forward to the future with hope and enthusiasm.
   b. I might as well give up because there is nothing I can do about making things better for myself.
   c. When things are going badly, I am helped by knowing that they cannot stay that way forever.
   d. I can't imagine what my life would be like in ten years.
   e. I have enough time to accomplish the things I want to do.
   f. In the future, I expect to succeed in what concerns me most.
   g. My future seems dark to me.
   h. I happen to be particularly lucky, and I expect to get more of the good things in life like than the average person.
   i. I just can't get the breaks, and there is no reason I will in the future.
   j. My past experiences have prepared me well for the future.
   k. All I can see ahead of me is unpleasantness rather than pleasantness.
   l. I don't expect to get what I really want.
   m. When I look ahead to the future, I expect that I will be happier than I am now.
   n. Things just won't work out the way I want them to.
   o. I have great faith in the future.
   p. I never get what I want, so its foolish to want anything.
   q. Its very unlikely that I will get any real satisfaction in the future.
   r. The future seems vague and uncertain to me.
   s. I can look forward to more good times than bad times.

t. There's no use in really trying to get anything I want because I probably won't get it.

9. Please answer the following. (Options: No, Sometimes, Yes)
   a. I have people in my life who I can respect
   b. I share/cooperate with people around me
   c. Getting and improving qualifications and skills is important to me
   d. I know how to behave in different social situations (such as at work, home, or other public places)
   e. My family is supportive towards me
   f. My family knows a lot about me (for example, who my friends are, what I like to do)
   g. If I am hungry, I can usually get enough food to eat.
   h. I try to finish activities that I start.
   i. Spiritual beliefs are a source of strength for me (for example, believing in God or Allah)
   j. I am proud of my ethnic background (for example, I am proud of where my family comes from or know a lot about my family's history).
   k. People think that I am fun to be with.
   l. I talk to my family/partner about how I feel (for example, when I am sad or concerned)
   m. When things don't go my way, I usually fix it without hurting myself or other people (e.g. without using drugs or being violent)
   n. I feel supported by my friends
   o. I know where to go if I need help
   p. I feel that I belong in my community
   q. My family cares about me when times are hard (for example, when I am ill or in trouble)
   r. My Friends cares about me when times are hard (for example, when I am ill or in trouble)
   s. I am treated fairly
   t. I have opportunities to show others that I can act responsibly
   u. I know what I am good at
   v. I participate in religious activities (like going to church or mosque)

w. I think it is important to help out in my community
x. I feel secure when I am with my family
y. I have opportunities to apply my abilities in life (like using skills, working at a job, or caring for others)
z. I like my family's culture and the way my family celebrates things (e.g. holidays)
aa. I like my community's culture and the way my community celebrates things (e.g. holidays or festivals)

10. Describe a time when someone else put pressure on you, and how you coped with it. (short answer question)

As published in Bazaar Magazine, Oct 2020

A Collectivist Society Examined: Developing Resilience During Crises in Kuwait

By Juliet Dinkha & Aya Abdulhadi

Keywords: Resilience, Coping, Collectivist Society, COVID-19, Crises

Introduction

It is during unprecedented times like now when we are presented with opportunities to conduct research to further understand the human behavioral psychology and interactions within a society. According to Psychology Today, Resilience is the psychological quality that allows some people to be knocked down by the adversities of life and come back at least as strong as before. Rather than letting difficulties, traumatic events, or failure overcome them and drain their resolve, highly resilient people find a way to change course, emotionally heal, and continue moving toward their goals (Psychology Today, 2020). Whether resilience is achieved or not is dependent on a number of factors influenced by the biological, social and psychological composition of the individual. Based on our study, we are outlining the essential coping skills developed and fostered by individuals in a collectivist society, Kuwait, to aid in processing their experience of the crisis and becoming resilient. The study was conducted during the spike of the COVID-19 pandemic in Kuwait and targeted young adults between the age of 18 and 25 and received 99 responses. Using multiple methodologies—library research, media collections, structured questionnaires —our research focuses on ten key questions about anxiety, depression, experience of the crises and how individuals are coping and lessons learned for the future, survey questions are included in the appendix section. Our combination of approaches allows us to gather social, and cultural contexts and meanings of young adults' attitudes, emotions, and actions as it relates to the pandemic and how this is contributing to their resilient self.

COVID-19 In Kuwait

With the spread of the virus across the world, Kuwait was one of the first countries to adopt measures and restrictions to fight the spread of the virus and to protect its national and non-nationals living in Kuwait. Stricter measures were enforced by the country, including governmental rules to suspend both public and private workplaces, schools and universities, amongst other institutions, to minimize physical interaction and maintain social distancing, which continued to be extended due to the spike of the situation in Kuwait. Furthermore, the government enforced a curfew to help in supporting minimizing the spread of the virus. With those different restrictions and changes to the normal life, the country's residents were exposed to unforeseen and unprecedented experiences. How did the public deal with this crises? How did this affect their current mindset and future views? What lessons have they learned and how did they learn to cope? These questions formulated the basis of our survey and hence our findings.

Developing Coping Skills & Being Resilient

During the pandemic, respondents resorted to engaging in various activities to help them become less anxious and depressed to overcome the alarming health risks posed by the spread of the pandemic and the social restriction enforced by the government. A total of 99 individuals answered the survey and an analysis of their responses revealed four main themes which highlighted how subjects dealt with the COVID-19 crisis and helped them develop resilience. The four themes conceptualized include (i) Cognitive Wellness; (ii) Interconnection to Self; (iii) Media Consumption and (iv) Social Support.

Cognitive Wellness

Respondents valued mental health and wellness and sought to achieve the same during the crises as a coping mechanism. Subjects reported examples which correlated with this theme including "taking tips from experts in psychology", "online therapy" and "staying positive". This mentality of directing their mind to such acts were developed by the individuals themselves to alter their personal experience of the crisis and the change this reflects on their self-processing of the events around them. Other respondents focused on including positive self-talk into their daily routine to keep themselves optimistic and foresee the upcoming events in a positive light.

Interconnection to Self

Another common theme across the answers received emphasized on the individual solely, where respondents continued to engage in personal hobbies and interests as a mechanism to cope with their growing anxiety levels and the challenging situation this pandemic presented them with. Although Kuwait is mainly identified as a collectivist society, respondents regulated oneself as an individual during the time of crisis, hence resorted to self-centered activities such as "baking", "reading", "exercising", "creating art", "journaling" and "watching series", amongst a number of other activities which are focused on the self. In order to foster resilience, one must be able to acknowledge the current adversary being experienced and try to develop the best mechanism or coping skills to be able to go through this adversary and become resilient. Our sample in this study followed this notion and started influencing their own selves and regulating their actions as a form of building resilience. Even the act of "online shopping" as reported by one of the respondents is a form of self-gratification and is practiced at an individual level.

Media Consumption

The flow of information is today's time is almost instant, especially with the rise of social media and immediate transformation transmitting. "Social media" was reported by a number of the respondents as one of the main coping mechanism they have found to have helped them cope with the developing pandemic. How media is consumed and what sentiments the audience are left with differs from a respondent to another. However, during a crisis in general, people would be more likely to try to look at the glass half full and not half empty, and this can be achieved by seeking both verified and positive news from official sources, and avoiding participating in the spread of rumors to support in limiting the negativity associated with its circulation. Correlating with this notion, our respondents reported that during the pandemic they have been doing the following: "keeping up to date with the latest verified news of the pandemic", "following social media accounts of the Ministry of Health", "trying not to read the news", "not spreading rumors" and "not reading fake news".

Social Support

Although during the pandemic, Kuwait was subjected to strict social distancing measures and curfews, around 80% of the respondents reported that they engaged with their family and friends as a measure to cope with the crises. Having access to one's social support system is a fundamental measure to cope with adversaries and become able to develop resilience towards such situation and that's because one feels the support and receives it to be able to overcome the hardship. Social interactions undertaken by our respondents were both direct and virtual. A number of the respondents mentioned that they were able to connect with their family and friends using the following methods: "talking to friends on the phone", "scheduled Zoom meeting with my friends once every few weeks", "family presence and support", "group video calls", "interacting with family members via WhatsApp" and "being around family".

Conclusion

The above listed coping skills were conceptualized based on the respondents' answers, which formed the basis for understating how the individuals in a collectivist society become resilient in times of crisis. Not only that resilience is evident to have been developed during crises, yet individuals were able to further foster their resilient self and envision a better future to be able to overcome the pandemic. Although a number of respondents have focused on nurturing individual hobbies and interests as their coping mechanisms, their presence in a collectivist society had helped them develop resilience during this pandemic. An advantage individuals have in a collectivist society is the immediate access to social support, mainly from family, due to the nature of the Kuwaiti society as a collectivist one, which encourages individuals to stay connected with their parents and family members, and in proximity as well, where individuals still continue to live in their parents' house. This immediate social support which is accessible during crises helps individuals in developing a resilient self, at the time of crisis and for other unforeseen circumstances.

References

Central Statistical Bureau. (2018). *Annual Statistical Abstract*. https://www.csb.gov.kw/Default_en

Gorodnichenko Y., Roland G. (2012) Understanding the Individualism-Collectivism Cleavage and Its Effects: Lessons from Cultural Psychology. In: Aoki M., Kuran T., Roland G. (eds) Institutions and Comparative Economic Development. International Economic Association Series. Palgrave Macmillan, London.

Psychology Today. (2020, April 9). *Resilience*. https://www.psychologytoday.com/us/basics/resilience

Appendix

Resilience

Survey on Resilience During Crises

In an effort to enhance the research on psychological responses to the current COVID-19 pandemic, examining the age group of 18 to 25, kindly complete the below survey with answers reflecting your feelings throughout the past 4-6 weeks. All answers will be treated confidentially. Please answer all the following *How anxious do you feel on a scale of 0 to10? (0 not anxious and 10 very anxious) and list at least 3 of your symptoms.*

1. **How depressed do you feel on a scale of 0 to 10? (0 not depressed and 10 very depressed) and list at least 3 of your symptoms.**
2. **How prepared did you feel in dealing with the pandemic (0 not ready at all, 10 very ready)**
3. **List at least three ways which are helping you deal with this crisis (i.e. social support)**
4. **List at least three ways you feel quarantine increased your stress during the crisis.**
5. **What advice would you have for someone who is not coping well during this time?**
6. **Please list your expectations for yourself as returning to your normal routine.**
7. **How has COVID-19 changed you as a person?**
8. **Do you feel the world will be different after the crisis ends? (Yes or No, please explain)**
9. **Please reflect on your experience to date. Are there some personal lessons you have learned during the COVID-19 pandemic? List at least three.**

As published in the International Journal of Social Sciences –Volume 8, Issue 1, 2013– Page 87.

The Effects of Gender and Culture on Coping Strategies: An Extension Study

Mourad Dakhli, Ph.D.
Juliet Dinkha, Psy.D.*
Monica Matta
Nisrine Aboul-Hosn, Psy.D.
American University of Kuwait
P.O. BOX 3323
SAFAT, 13034
KUWAIT
jdinkha@auk.edu.kw
+(965) 1802040 ext. 435

*Contact Person

Abstract

Previous research suggests that gender differences exist in coping strategies of undergraduate students with significant effects on various affective and instrumental outcomes including self-esteem. For example, Lawrence (2006) reveals that there is a significant difference between males and females in terms of engagement in coping strategies and academic attainment. These results show that compared to females, males tend to detach themselves from the emotions of a situation and select different coping strategies. This study is an extension of the existing research as it investigates differences in coping strategies adopted by students in a collectivist society. The aim of this paper is to explore differences of the various coping strategies within gender in Kuwait. We also compare our results to those previously reported in the

United States, and individualist society.

We use survey methodology to collect data from young students attending various schools in Kuwait. A well-established Coping Strategies survey was administered to test a set of hypotheses related to the various types of coping mechanisms including the use of religion, social support, and denial. We hope to shed more light on the role of gender in employing a given coping strategy. We discuss our results, their implications for theory and practice, and propose directions for further research in this important area.

Keywords: Coping Strategies, Self-Esteem, Gender Differences, Collectivist Society, Religion

Introduction And Review

According to Piko (2001) "coping encompasses the cognitive and behavioral strategies where the individual is able to manage stressful situations and the negative emotion reactions elicited by that event." Due to the broad definition of coping (Cooper & Dewe, 2004), the research on the topic is one that is wide yet lacking in light of the multitude of factors that impact the selection of coping mechanisms.

Limited studies have explored the interplay between gender differences and coping strategies outside the context of North America. With the increasing focus on cultural diversity and the need to understand individuals within their mainstream culture, this paper aims to minimize the gap in the literature and hopes to shed light on the various coping strategies utilized by male and female adolescents living in Kuwait, and in turn how such selected strategies impact self esteem.

In order to enhance the understanding of the interplay between coping strategies, gender and culture, Olah's (1995) three-A parcel theory will be utilized. The three-A parcel theory divides commonly used coping strategies into one of three domains: Assimilation, Accommodation, and Avoidance. Olah (1995) postulates that assimilative coping strategies involve cognitive and behavioral attempts on the individual's part to change his/her environment, while accommodation coping strategies involve cognitive and behavioral attempts on the individual's part to change himself/herself as part of environmental adaptation, and finally avoidance coping strategies entail cognitive and behavioral efforts to physically and/or psychologically disconnect. (p. 495-496)

Our current paper will attempt to group the strategies outlined by Craver (1989) in the COPE questionnaire into Olah's three-A parcels. Specifically the paper postulates that a) positive reinterpretation and growth, b) instrumental social support, c) active coping, and d) planning can be considered Assimilative coping strategies, while a) religious coping, b) humor, c) emotional social support, d) acceptance, and e) restraint are considered Accommodative coping techniques, and finally a) mental disengagement, b) focus on and venting of emotions, c) denial, d) behavioral disengagement, e) substance abuse, and f) suppression of competing activities are grouped under the Avoidance coping strategies. The paper thus attempts to broaden conclusions regarding individual utility of coping strategies within a specific cultural setting, that of adolescents living in Kuwait.

Adolescence

Adolescence is a critical transitional developmental period, as it entails a multitude of factors that interplay and impact identity development (Compas, Orosan, & Grant, 1993; Compas, Malcarne, & Fondacaro, 1988). According to Plancherel et.al (1998), adolescence "is characterized by transitions in many areas, hormonal and physical changes accompanied by cognitive developments (beginning of abstract thinking and theorization) as well as social affective changes (sexual relationships, self-esteem, locus of control and autonomy from parents). The implementation of effective coping strategies, during this phase, is essential as it has a long-term impact on mental health, interpersonal relationships, and one's self esteem (Dumont & Provost, 1999). This matter is further complicated by socio-cultural factors that prescribe normative gender roles, application of coping mechanisms and manifestation of emotional and cognitive needs.

Many adolescents have not explored the meaning of their ethnicity. Moreover, if these young people have internalized negative societal stereotypes of their ethnic group, they are likely to experience lower self-esteem and self-confidence, and they may have difficulty in finding meaning in their lives (Dinkha, Abdulhamid, 2008).

As it pertains to the current study, it is expected that the interdependent nature of the Kuwaiti family and society will likely impact adolescent development in terms of reduced autonomy, continued need for emotional support, decreased self reliance, and problematic decision making. Adolescents living in Kuwait, given that the individual is an extension of the family, learn that family is the source of support and also the forum in which problems are resolved. Moreover, gender roles are an imminent factor in how problems are expressed, emotions are manifested, and support is sought.

In essence, given the patriarchal nature of Kuwaiti society and the Islamic regulations regarding female social outlets, it is predicted that females will more likely utilize social support for emotional reasons. On the other hand, males will likely utilize denial as a coping mechanism to stay in accord with prescribed male gender norms and roles. This is especially the case with regards to the need to manage impressions imposed by societal and religious sanctions. Despite such predicted differences in the utility of coping mechanisms, religion is expected to be an overarching and underlying catalyst. Indeed, researchers of religious coping have found that Muslims commonly engage in religious coping when faced with challenges in their daily lives (Ali, Peterson & Huang, 2003; Eapan & Reveesz, 2003; Errihani et al., 2008). Several researchers have also reported a positive association between Islamic religiosity and well being, happiness, life satisfaction, and general mental health (Abdel-Khalek, 2006; Abdel Khalek, 2007; Abdel Khalek, 2008).

It therefore is anticipated that adolescents living in Kuwait will utilize a combination of assimilative, accommodative, and avoidance coping strategies depending on the scope of established gender roles, family values, and religious orientation. However, given the prevalence of uniform cultural, religious and familial values, accommodative coping strategies are predicted to be utilized more often

Our discussion of the cultural, religious, and social context in Kuwait lead us to the following hypotheses:

1. Respondents in Kuwait will rely more on accommodative coping strategies.
2. Religion will be an important coping strategy given the role of religion in the Kuwaiti society.
3. Females will select seeking social support and emotion-based strategies or emotional reasons more than males.
4. Denial, as a coping strategy, will be utilized more by males due to greater restrictions by the society on their personal expressions.

Methods, Results & Discussion

For the purpose of this study we used the full COPE questionnaire (Carver et al., 1989). The COPE questionnaire is a 60-item measure designed to evaluate the different coping mechanisms people use in response to stress (Carver et al., 1989). It uses the 15 scales that are defined below:

1. *Positive reinterpretation and growth;* making the best of the situation by growing from it or viewing it in a more favorable light.
2. *Instrumental social support;* seeking assistance, information, or advice about what to do.
3. *Active coping;* taking action or exerting efforts to remove or circumvent the stressor.
4. *Planning;* thinking about how to confront the stressor, planning one's active coping efforts.
5. *Religious coping;* increased engagement in religious activities.
6. *Humor;* making jokes about the stressor.
7. *Emotional social support;* getting sympathy or emotional support from someone.
8. *Acceptance;* accepting the fact that the stressful event has occurred

and is real.
9. *Restraint*; coping passively by holding back one's coping attempts until they can be of use.
10. *Mental disengagement*; psychological disengagement from the goal with which the stressor is interfering, through daydreaming, sleep, or self-distraction.
11. *Focus on and venting of emotions*; an increased awareness of one's emotional distress, and a concomitant tendency to ventilate or discharge those feelings.
12. *Denial*; an attempt to reject the reality of the stressful event.
13. *Behavioral disengagement*; giving up, or withdrawing effort from, the attempt to attain the goal with which the stressor is interfering.
14. *Substance abuse*; turning to the use of alcohol and other drugs as a way of disengaging from the stressor.
15. *Suppression of competing activities*; suppressing one's attention to other activities in which one might engage in order to concentrate more completely on dealing with the stressor (Taylor, 1998)

In this study we used the stratified random sampling method. Male and female adolescents, between the ages of 13 to 18, studying at various schools in Kuwait, were administered the COPE comprehensive questionnaire. A group of university students were trained by the lead researches on valid and reliable means to administer the COPE survey.

We collected data from 259 students from various high schools. The sample was evenly divided between males and females.

About 23% of the respondents were between ages 13-14, 34.6% were aged 15-16, and 17.9% were 17 year-olds or higher.

We performed a set of independent samples t-tests to investigate the role of gender differences on coping mechanisms. The results are summarized in Table 1 below.

Table 1: Coping Mechanisms Differences between Gender

Coping Mechanism	t-value	p-value	Males	Females
Positive Reinterpretation (PR)	-1.7	0.09	2.91	3.00
Mental Disengagement (MD)*	-2.985	0.003*	2.65	2.83
Focus on and Venting of Emotions (EM)*	-3.887	0*	2.55	2.78
Instrumental Social Support (ISS)*	-3.439	0.001*	2.79	2.99
Active Coping (AC)	-0.049	0.961	2.82	2.82
Denial (D)	0.209	0.835	2.20	2.18
Religious Coping (RC)*	-2.208	0.028*	3.03	3.14
Humor (H)	0.446	0.656	2.42	2.40
Behavioral Disengagement (BD)	-1.776	0.076	2.04	2.14
Restraint (R)	-0.9	0.369	2.63	2.68
Emotional Social Support (ESS)*	-2.838	0.005*	2.59	2.80
Substance Use (SU)	1.445	0.149	1.46	1.38
Acceptance (A)	-1.133	0.258	2.81	2.86
Suppression of Competing Activities (SCA)	-1.393	0.164	2.58	2.65
Planning (P)	-1.245	0.214	2.87	2.93

- *Significant at 0.05.*

Discussion

We postulated earlier that in our context, coping mechanisms that rely on outside support and societal variables will be dominant given the collectivist and religious nature of the Kuwaiti society. We have also suggested that due to strict gender roles, females will rely more on emotion-based or accommodative type strategies (Frydenberg & Lewis, 1993; Radford, Mann, Ohta, & Nakane, 1993). Our results show that both genders use various coping strategies as a mechanism to deal with stressful situations. We found a significant difference (p≤ .05) in the use of these coping strategies between males and female respondents. As would be expected based on our discussion of the Kuwaiti social context, females relied on coping strategies more than did their male counterparts, and were more likely to seek outside social support.

The main findings of our study center around two themes. First, accommodative strategies were dominant for both males and females. This, we argue is to a large part due to the collectivist context where acceptance of societal norms, subordination of self-interest for that of the collective, and the importance of religion are important factors that shape perceptions and behaviors (Kagitcibasi, 1997; Triandis, 1995; Kawanishi, 1995). In contrast, and as was found in various studies completed in North America, a region where individualism is in general high (Hofstede, 2001), coping strategies were found to be more focused on internal mechanisms that were related to greater tendency and need for independence and control .

Second, our results were in line with previous research whereby females tended to seek more external sources of support and were less likely to engage in denial or other strategies deemed less effective in coping with stressful situations (Renk & Creasey, 2003). In particular, females were less likely to resort to denial or substance abuse in managing stressful situations. Females also tended to use humor less than males as a coping mechanism though the results were not conclusive for these variables. Nonetheless, the overall average score for the avoidance strategies was lower for females than for males.

It is interesting to note that the ranking of the coping strategies were similar for both genders whereby assimilation was the most widely used strategy, followed by accommodation, then avoidance. Assimilation, which includes the use of instrumental social support, positive reinterpretation, and planning, may have been the highest due to the type of sample used. The sample was made-up of adolescents between the ages of 14 and 18, and for such age groups self efficacy may be higher, and respondents may feel that there is ample time for things to get better.

As expected, the results indicated that religious coping was utilized by both genders. In fact, religion was found to be the most prominent coping strategy employed by both males and females with females more frequently reporting religion as a mean to manage stressful situations.

Our results have implications for both research and practice. On the research side, a more systematic investigation of coping mechanisms in different societal contexts is needed. Individuals are constantly managing and reacting to societal pressures. Norms, values, and societal expectations were shown to vary across various cultural values including individualism-collectivism, power distance, risk avoidance and others (Copeland, & Hess, 1995; Ward, & Kennedy, 2001). It has been shown that these cultural variables will have an impact on the perceptions, attitudes, and behaviors of individuals. Consequently, it is expected that coping strategies will also be contingent on societal culture as well as individual orientations.

On the practical side, counseling and support services should be cognizant of the various coping strategies adopted, and the role of gender and culture in affecting such strategies. Intervention mechanisms within or outside organizations can be that much more effective and successful if they take into consideration both the individual variables (e.g. gender, age, etc.), and societal factors (culture, social structure, etc.).

To conclude, societies all over the world are constantly developing and evolving, leading to previous static variables becoming increasingly dynamic. Kuwait is one of these societies, that as a whole is undergoing its own identity re-development. Hence, the individuals within this society are themselves adapting and progressing. Future research should likely focus on the capacities and capabilities of individuals to successfully attain a healthy balance between societal and individual pressures, and how such a balance can further promote healthy psychological functioning.

Appendix A. Coping Survey Items

(PR) Positive reinterpretation and growth
- I try to grow as a person as result of the experience.
- I try to see it in a different light, to make it seem more positive.
- I look for something good in what is happening.
- I learn something from the experience.

(MD) Mental disengagement
- I turn to work or other substitute activities to take my mind off things.
- I daydream about things other than this.
- I sleep more than usual.
- I go to movies or watch TV, to think about it less.

(EM) Focus on and venting of emotions
- I get upset and let my emotions out.
- I get upset, and am really aware of it.
- I let my feelings out.
- I feel a lot of emotional distress and I find myself expressing those feelings a lot.

(ISS) Use of instrumental social support
- I try to get advice from someone about what to do.
- I talk to someone to find out more about the situation.
- I talk to someone who could do something concrete about the problem.
- I ask people who have had similar experiences what they did.

(AC) Active coping
- I concentrate my efforts on doing something about it.
- I take additional action to try to get rid of the problem.
- I take direct action to get around the problem.
- I do what has to be done, one step at a time.

(D) Denial
- I say to myself "this isn't real."
- I refuse to believe that it had happened.
- I pretend that it hasn't really happened.
- I act as though it hasn't even happened.

(RC) Religious coping
- I put my trust in God.
- I seek God's help
- I try to find comfort in my religion.
- I pray more than usual.

(H) Humor
- I make jokes about it.
- I kid around about it
- I make fun of the situation.
- I laugh about the situation

(BD) Behavioral disengagement
- I just give up trying to reach my goal.
- I give up the attempt to get what I want.
- I admit to myself that I can't deal with it, and quit trying.
- I reduce the amount of effort I'm putting into solving the problem.

(R) Restraint
- I restrain myself from doing anything too quickly.
- I hold off doing anything
- about it until the situation permits.
- I make sure not to make matters worse by acting too soon.
- I force myself to wait for the right time to do something.

(ESS) Use of emotional social support
- I try to get emotional support from friends or relatives.
- I talk to someone about how I feel.

- I discuss my feelings with someone.
- I get sympathy and understanding from someone.

(SU) Substance use
- I use alcohol or drugs to make myself feel better.
- I try to lose myself for a while by drinking alcohol or taking drugs.
- I drink alcohol or take drugs, in order to think about it less.
- I use alcohol or drugs to help me get through it.

(A) Acceptance
- I get used to the idea that it happened.
- I accept that this has happened and that it can't be changed.
- I accept the reality of the fact that it happened.
- I learn to live with it.

(SCA) Suppression of competing activities
- I keep myself from getting distracted by other thoughts or activities.
- I focus on dealing with this problem, and if necessary let other things slide a little.
- I try hard to prevent other things from interfering with my efforts at dealing with this.
- I put aside other activities in
- In order to concentrate on this.

(P) Planning
- I make a plan of action.
- I try to come up with a strategy about what to do.
- I think about how I might best handle the problem.
- I think hard about what step to take.

References

Abdel-Khalek, A. M. (2006). Happiness, health, and religiosity: Significant relations. *Mental Health, Religion & Culture, 9*(1), 85–97.

Abdel-Khalek, A. M. (2007). Religiosity, happiness, health and psychopathology in a probability sample of Muslim adolescents. *Mental Health, Religion and Culture, 10*, 571-583.

Ai, A., Peterson, C., & Huang, B. (2003). The effect of religious-spiritual coping on positive attitudes of adult Muslim refugees from Kosovo and Bosnia. *International Journal for the Psychology of Religion, 13*(1), 29-47.

Ajrouch, K.J. (2000). Place, age, and culture: Community living and ethnic identity among Lebanese American adolescents. *Small Group Research, 31*, 447– 469.

Bardi, A. & Guerra, V. M. (2011). Cultural Values Predict Coping Using Culture as an Individual Difference Variable in Multicultural Samples. *Journal of Cross-Cultural Psychology, 42*(6), 908-927. doi: 10.1177/0022022110381119

Carver, C. S., Scheier, M. F., & Weintraub, J. K. (1989). Assessing coping strategies: A theoretically based approach. *Journal of Personality and Social Psychology, 56*, 267-283.

CIA Web Site — Central Intelligence Agency. (n.d.). The World Factbook - Kuwait. Retrieved November 16, 2010, from https://www.cia.gov/library/publications/the-world-factbook/geos/ku.html

Compas, B. E., Malcarne, V. L., & Fondacaro, K. M. (1988). Coping with stressful events in older children and young adolescents. *Journal of Consulting and Clinical Psychology, 56*(3), 405-411. doi: 10.1037/0022-006X.56.3.405

mpas, B. E., Orosan, P. G., & Grant, K. E. (1993). Adolescent stress and coping: Implications for psychopathology during adolescence. *Journal of Adolescence, 16*(3), 331-349. doi: 10.1006/jado.1993.1028

Compas, B. E., Connor-Smith, J. K., Saltzman, H., Thomsen, A. H., & Wadsworth, M. E. (2001). Coping with stress during childhood and adolescence: Problems, progress and potential in theory and research. *Psychological Bulletin,* 127.

Constantine, M. G., Donnelly, P. C., & Myers, L. J. (2002). Collective self-esteem and africultural coping styles in African American adolescents. *Journal of Black Studies, 32,* 698.

Copeland, E. P. & Hess, R. S. (1995). Differences in Young Adolescents' Coping Strategies Based On Gender and Ethnicity. *The Journal of Early Adolescence, 15*(2), 203-219. doi: 10.1177/0272431695015002002

Dinkha, J., Abdulhamid, S., & Abdelhalim, N. (2008). How Identity Is Constructed: An Analysis of Four Case Studies. *Psychology Journal, 4,* (5).

Dumont, M. & Provost, M. A. (1999). Resilience in adolescents: Protective role of social support, coping strategies, self-esteem, and social activities on experience of stress and depression. *Journal of Youth and Adolescence, 28*(3), 343-363.

Dwairy, M. & Van Sickle, T. (1996). Western psychotherapy in traditional Arabic societies. *Clinical Psychology Review, 16*(3), 231-249.

Dwairy, M. (1998). *Cross cultural psychotherapy: The Arab Palestinian case;* New York: Haworth Press.

Eapen, V., Revesz, T. (2003). Psychosocial correlates of paediatric cancer in the United Arab Emirates, *Supportive Care in Cancer, 11,* 185-189.

El Alami, D. S. & Hinchcliffe, D. (1996). Islamic Marriage and Divorce Laws of the Arab World 3.

Socioeconomic Factors of the Family. (2009). In *Encyclopedia Britannica*. Retrieved from

Errihani, H., Mrabti, H., Boutayeb, S., El Ghissassi, I., El Mesbahi, O., Hammoudi, M., Chergui, H., Riadi, A. (2008). Impact of cancer on Moslem patients in Morocco, *Psycho-Oncology, 17*(1), 98-100.

Fewell, R. R. (1986). Supports from religious organizations and personal beliefs. In R. R. Fewell & P. F. Vadasy (Eds.). *Families of handicapped children: Needs and supports across the life span* (pp. 297-316). Austin: Pro-Ed.

Frydenberg, E. & Lewis, R. (1993). Boys play sport and girls turn to others: Age, gender and ethnicity as determinants of coping. Journal of Adolescence, 16(3), 253-266. doi: 10.1006/jado.1993.1024

Hofstede, G. (1991). *Culture and organizations: Software of the mind.* London: McGraw-Hill.

Hofstede G. (2001). *Comparing values, behaviors, institutions, and organizations across nations.* 2nd edn. Sage Publications; Thousand Oaks, CA: 2001. Culture's consequences.

Holahan, C. J., & Moos, R. H. (1987). Risk, resistance, and psychological distress: A longitudinal analysis with adults and children. *Journal of Abnormal Psychology, 96,* 3-13.

Holahan, C. J., Moos, R. H., Holoahan, C. K., Cronkite, R. C. & Randall, P. K. (2001). Drinking to cope, emotional distress and alcohol use and abuse: a ten year model. *J. Stud. Alcohol, 62,* 190-198.

Kagitcibasi, C. (1997). Individualism and collectivism. In J. W. Berry, M. H., Segall, & G. Kagitcibasi, (Eds.), 2nd ed., *Handbook of cross-cultural psychology, 3,* 1-49. Boston, MA: Allyn & Bacon.

Kawanishi, Y. (1995). The effects of culture on beliefs about stress and coping: Causal attribution of Anglo-American and Japanese persons. *Journal of Contemporary Psychotherapy, 25*(1), 49-60. doi: 10.1007/BF02308668

Kuo, B. C. H. (2010). Culture's Consequences on Coping Theories, Evidences, and Dimensionalities. *Journal of Cross-Cultural Psychology, 42*(6), 1084-1100. doi: 10.1177/0022022110381126

Kuwait Government, Ministry of Planning. (2005). Statistics and Census Sector. Summary Findings of the Preliminary Results of the Population Census of Kuwait, 2005. Retrieved November 16, 2010.

Kuwait Government Online. (2008). Population of Kuwait. http://www.e.gov.kw/sites/KGoEnglish/Portal/Pages/PortalMain.aspx

Lawrence, J. (2006, July). Engaging first year students: a collaborative approach implemented in a first year nursing course. Paper presented at the 9th Pacific Rim Conference - First Year in Higher Education: Engaging Students, Gold Coast, Australia. Retrieved from http://eprints.usq.edu.au/archive/00000983/

Nobles, A. and Sciarra, D. (2000). Cultural Determinants in the treatment of Arab Americans: A primer for mainstream therapists. *American Journal of Orthopsychiatry, 70,* 182-191.

Olah, A., (1995). Coping strategies among adolescents: a cross-cultural study. *Journal of Adolescence, 18,* 491-512.

Ongen, D. E. (2006). The relationships between self-criticism, submissive behavior and depression among Turkish adolescents. *Personality Individual Differences, 41,* 793-800.

Perosa, S. L., & Perosa, L. M. (1993). Relationships among Minuchin's structural family model, identity achievement, and coping style. *Journal of Counseling Psychology, 40* (4), 479-489.

Piko, B. (2001). Gender differences and similarities on adolescents' ways of coping. *Psychological Record, 51,* 223-235.

Plancherel, B., Bolognini, M. y Halfon, O. (1998). Coping strategies in early and mid adolescence: Difference according to age and gender in a community sample. *European Psychologist, 3*(3), 192-201.

Ptacek, J. T., Smith, R. E., & Dodge, K. L. (1994). Gender differences in coping with stress: When stressor and appraisal do not differ. *Personality and Social Psychology Bulletin, 20,* 421–430.

Radford, M. H. B., Mann, L., Ohta, Y., & Nakane, Y. (1993). Differences between Australian and Japanese Students in Decisional Self-Esteem, Decisional Stress, and Coping Styles. *Journal of Cross-Cultural Psychology, 24*(3), 284-297. doi: 10.1177/0022022193243002

Renk, K. and Creasey, G. 2003. The relationship of gender, gender identity, and coping strategies in late adolescence. *Journal of late adolescence, 26,* 159-168.

Rosenberg, M. (1965). *Society and the adolescent self-image.* Princeton, NJ: Princeton University Press.

Safra Project. (n.d.). Sexuality, Gender and Islam. Safra Project. Retrieved November 17, 2010, from http://www.safraproject.org/sgi-intro.htm

Stouffer, Samuel A., Edward A. Suchman, Leland C. DeVinney, Shirley A. Star, and Robin M. Williams. 1965. The American Soldier: Adjustment During Army Life. New York: Science Editions.

Stouffer, S. A., Lumsdaine, A. A., Lumsdaine, M. H., Williams, R. M., Smith, M. B., Janis, I. L., et al. (1965). *The American Soldier: Combat and Its Aftermath*. New York: Science Editions.

Taylor, S. E., Pham, L. B., Rivkin, I. D., & Armor, D. A. (1998). Harnessing the imagination: Mental simulation, self-regulation, and coping. *American Psychologist, 53*(4), 429-439.

Torstrick, R. L., & Faier, E. (2009). Gender, marriage, and family. In *Culture and customs of the Arab Gulf States* (p. 112). Westport, CT: Greenwood Press.

Triandis, H. C. (1995). *Individualism and collectivism*. Boulder, CO: Westview.

Ward, C. & Kennedy, A. (2001). Coping with Cross-Cultural Transition. *Journal of Cross-Cultural Psychology, 32*(5), 636-642. doi: 10.1177/0022022101032005007

CHAPTER 5

Closing Remarks

THE FACTORS AFFECTING one's identity are myriad and because of how our similarities set each one of us apart, the search for the social identity continues by our younger self. How our beliefs are constructed and how much of influence we allow onto them from our everyday activities could lead each one of us in different paths. Societies evolve when its individuals evolve and share their identities together, even if they tend to practice a more individualistic sense of themselves in their society. The trajectory of how societies advances is bound to the affecting nature of many of its constituting factors, and mainly the individuals themselves. In this case, the youth and young adults are changing norms in society and reflexively are also influencing their own socialization and identity construction. Both males and females in the society will create identities that will see their own light yet away and close from each other depending on how each allows the controlling forces of the society to contribute to their identity building. Today's media scene is no longer one comprised of only local or Arab content as many youth, young adults and adults continue to consume Western media content. As with this quest for identity continues and will continue to be influenced by how much the individuals allow themselves to be immersed in virtual circles and how this reflects on their identity, especially when many are forging friendships beyond Kuwait, in other countries or through social media platforms. Social identities and their interaction is a vast field for research, and with every new media channel emerging, new realizations about the self are unveiled. Also, whether individuals reveal their true identities or only a fraction of it will continue to drive research in the field of social psychology, since the power of the slightest change in one state could ripple differences around the globe, as with the flapping wings of a butterfly.

References

AlMatrouk, L. (2016). The relationship between gender segregation in schools, self-esteem, spiritual values/religion, and peer relations in Kuwait. *Near and Middle Eastern Journal of Research in Education, 2016*(1), 3.

Alsuwailan, Z. F. (2006). *The impact of societal values on Kuwaiti women and the role of* education*. The University of Tennessee.

Bazaar, Dinkha, J., & Abdulhamid, A. (2020). *A COLLECTIVIST SOCIETY EXAMINED: Developing Resilience During Crises In Kuwait*. Bazaar.town | the Ultimate Guide to Kuwait. https://bazaar.town/a-collectivist-society-examined/

Crystal, J. (1992). Kuwait: the Transformation of an Oil State (1st ed.). Routledge. https://doi.org/10.4324/9781315628776

Dakhli, M., Dinkha, J., Matta, M., & Aboul-Hosn, N. (2013). The effects of gender and culture on coping strategies: an extension study. *International Journal of Social Sciences, 8*(1), 87.

Dinkha, J. (2014). The Relationship Among TV Violence, Aggression, Anti-Social Behaviors and Parental Mediation. *Mediterranean Journal of Social Sciences*, 5(23), 1906-1913. https://doi.org/10.5901/mjss.2014.v5n23p1906

Dinkha, J., Abdulhadi, A., Al-Kandari, A., & Al-Obaid, S. (2021). Navigating through Resilience: Young Adults in Kuwait. *ATHENS JOURNAL OF MEDITERRANEAN STUDIES*, 8(1), 49–66. https://doi.org/10.30958/ajms.8-1-3

Dinkha, J., Mitchel, C., Dakhil, M. (2015). Attachment Styles and Parasocial Relationships: A Collectivist Society Perspective. In B. Mohan (Ed.) *Construction of Social Psychology* (Ch 10, pp. 105-121). InScience Press.

Dinkha, J. ., Mitchell, C. ., Rose, J. ., Rashwan, T. ., & Matta, M. . (2010). Altruism and Social Learning in Kuwait; an Analysis of Gender Differences. *Journal of Educational and Social Research*, 2(6), 97-104. https://www.richtmann.org/journal/index.php/jesr/article/view/12040

Dinkha, J., Mitchell, C., Zogheib, B., & Abdulhadi, A. (2022). The Online Looking Glass: The Study of Self Esteem and Narcissism on Instagram within a Patriarchal and Collectivist Society. *ATHENS JOURNAL OF SOCIAL SCIENCES*, 9(3), 273–296. https://doi.org/10.30958/ajss.9-3-4

Dinkha, J., Mobasher, S. (2012). The Risk of Depression and Suicide Among the University Students of Kuwait: A Cross-Study of Three Universities. *Psychology and Education*, 49(1&2) 7-18.

Dinkha, J., Mobasher, S., & El- Shamsy, N. (2010). Psychological Impact of Gender Segregation. *Psychology and Education*, 47(1&2), 23-34.

Ghys, É. (2013). The Lorenz attractor, a paradigm for chaos. *Chaos*, 1-54.

Hagger, M. S., Rentzelas, P., & Koch, S. (2014). Evaluating group member behaviour under individualist and collectivist norms: A cross-cultural comparison. *Small Group Research*, 45(2), 217-228.

Islam, G. (2014). Social identity theory. *Journal of personality and Social Psychology*, 67, 741-763.

Kemp, S. (2022). *DataReportal*. DataReportal. https://datareportal.com/reports/digital-2022-kuwait?rq=Kuwait

Mitchell, C., Dinkha, J., Kononova, A., & Matta, M. (2014). A Body of Dissatisfaction: a Study of the Effects of Media Imperialism in Kuwait. *American Journal of Humanities and Social Sciences*, 2(1), 76-87. https://doi.org/10.11634/232907811402471

Oyserman, D., & Uskul, A. K. (2015). Individualism and collectivism: Societal-level processes with implications for individual-level and society-level outcomes. In *Multilevel analysis of individuals and cultures* (pp. 145-173). Psychology Press.

Tajfel, H., & Turner, J. C. (2004). The social identity theory of intergroup behavior. In *Political psychology* (pp. 276-293). Psychology Press.

The Public Authority For Civil Information. (2022, June). Gender By Nationality and Age and Governate. Paci.gov.kw. http://stat.paci.gov.kw/englishreports/

Triandis, H. (1988). Collectivism v. individualism: A reconceptualisation of a basic concept in cross-cultural social psychology. In *Cross-cultural studies of personality, attitudes and cognition* (pp. 60-95). Palgrave Macmillan, London.

Turner, J. C., Hogg, M. A., Oakes, P. J., Reicher, S. D., & Wetherell, M. S. (1987). *Rediscovering the social group: A self-categorization theory*. basil Blackwell.

Wheeler, D. (2000). New media, globalization and Kuwaiti national identity. *Middle East Journal, 54*(3, The Information Revolution), pp. 432-444.

CPSIA information can be obtained
at www.ICGtesting.com
Printed in the USA
BVHW052318050223
657834BV00013B/2125